ANXIETY & DEPRESSION - A JOURNEY FROM SUFFERING TO THRIVING

An inspiring story of a Mental Health Warrior

PROF. (DR.) USHA DABAS

To a very special person in my life,

MY BELOVED FATHER

who left for his heavenly abode before completion of this book.

Amidst Tribulations and challenges of life,
the glory and gloom of enigmatic existence,
he cultivated Never Say Die attitude in me
and made me what I am today.

I'll see you at the crossroads-
You hold
a special place in my heart,
For Eternity.

"Mental health problems don't define who you are. They are something you experience. You walk in the rain and you feel the rain, but, importantly, YOU ARE NOT THE RAIN." -- Matt Haig

DON'T GIVE UP!

BE YOUR OWN SUNSHINE!

PROF.(DR) USHA DABAS

CONTENTS

PREFACE

"While going through the hell, keep going." I'd read somewhere. "There would be definitely a light at the end of that wicked tunnel", I added to the statement with a confident grin after learning the story of Dr. Liza Fernandez who despite being a Psychiatrist herself, suffered from mental health issues, but fought successfully and recovered from her condition due to her strong determination and resolve to prevail over it.

"YOUR MIND IS THE WORST ENEMY OF YOURS"—Someone suffering from chronic anxiety disorder told me once, while narrating her physical and mental struggle for survival. I realized essence of the statement through Dr. Liza's story and got the reason to write this book.

Learning life lessons and growing are emotional phenomena and often painful experiences. Sometimes, things happen in life that we've neither planned nor expected. Psychological trauma can leave us struggling with hurtful emotions, memories, and anxiety that will not go away. It can leave us feeling dull, disconnected, and distrustful. Irrespective of the cause, when we go through a painful, undesirable or traumatic experience, that experience can only become one of two things to us—it may become a long-term problem, or it may become our core strength. They may either make us or break us forever. However, they are inevitable and vital parts of our life.

Writing this book was a challenging task for me. It was an intricate job to collect real data, right data and vital details to include, be a good listener, tap into emotions, suitably condense or expand the story, privacy protection of actual characters and create a set of easily-visualizable scenes for a reader to experience the depth of the story, to list a few. Plunging into few years' painful memories was indeed a daunting task for Dr. Liza, I admit. We started from the beginning, blowing dust off old memories, extracting them from the depth of her mind. As we dug, the memories started to flow rapidly with greater ease. She remained fully immersed in her narrative and ably provided exact body to this story. I did my best to stay neutral, and not too sentimental, but it wasn't always easy. I've tried to amiably inject my perspectives too into the writing, while retaining sanctity and purity of the story. Hence, the readers will find the book as written in the narrator's own words.

While writing this book, I got a new lens to look at my own life. I saw new details that never occurred to me. I was able to discover myself and about the lives of other characters of this story.

In 2021, we are in midst of a worldwide COVID19 pandemic, with uncertainty, plight, and predicaments causing mental health issues for significant population globally. It is challenging to navigate this uncertainty, social separation, and fear psychosis. Hence, in the face of this unique crisis, it is very vital to manage our anxiety, fears, depression, and stress and maintain mental health along with physical health., I hope this inspiring and motivating book will constructively benefit the people affected by mental stress and anxiety and will make them able to take steps to regain control of their mental and physical health.

In life there are always undesirable things, so in order to feel better we just require looking at the life from another angle. However big the problem may be, life is certainly bigger than that! Every cloud has a silver line. So, it's desired to be positive and stay optimistic in every situation. By exploring life of someone through my writing, I was able to explore my own life. I feel happy that I was able to give voice to the story of someone, showing that I understand her and her story, dive into it, explore its depths and share it with the world.

INTRODUCTION

A best gift a writer can give to the world is to tell someone else's story. Writing someone else's story isn't an easy task, though, especially, when it's about psychological struggle of a psychiatry professor! Also, while writing for others, you've to capture your subject's voice, feelings and experiences precisely so as to give best justice to the story. You've to be a confidant, trusted friend with great listening and interviewing skills. It's tough and emotional work. It's amazingly satisfying, though.

Recollecting traumatic, sad and distressing memories from past, rekindling them through a series of events, serially binding in a pattern and reliving them can't be pleasant for anyone. However, as per legendary Shakespeare's philosophy, we must play our roles in the best of our capacity and potential on this world stage, defying all our challenges so as to make the life prolific and worth living. Learning lessons from our own experiences and those of others and moving on in life is an important process for a healthy, contented life. In fact, we remain the same person emotionally until we learn our lesson. Some experiences keep haunting us time and time again. I know the people who had rough experiences as kids or adolescents who are still subconsciously playing out the same emotional experiences from past episodes. They still feel the same scare or exuberance of those experiences. They haven't learned or changed since that event. Such experiences have incredible power to ruin the life and destroy the person. Hence, we shall not want our traumatic or negative experiences to become our lifelong weakness.

As a matter of fact, Depression, Anxiety and panic attacks ain't the signs of weakness, but the signs of having tried to remain strong for long. Most of us, perhaps every one of us, has either gone through this at some point in our lives or may be going through in present. When life is moving in an undesirable direction and the things are really bad, having meaning and purpose in life gives us something to hold on to. It is very imperative and humane to share the care, concern, compassion and support, and let those who struggle know that they're not alone in the battle of graceful survival, but they have strength of people supporting them, who empathize with them, who love, care and have concern for them. Although, it's really hard to explicate and console the aching and traumatized hearts, it also takes courage to overcome dark places one may end up in life. It requires confidence, self-control, faith, and strength of the people who love us sincerely to pull us through tough times.

Scientific studies report that when we feel a powerfully emotional experience, we observe what is known as a "refractory period"—which is our physiological response to our experience, which should be short to recover rapidly, without much psychological impact on our life. Often people don't cope well with their experiences, though. At times, refractory period of certain experiences may last for many months or even years with great power and potential to change us. Good and bad experiences have direct effect upon our living and lives. Nostalgia with good memories are pleasurable and energy boosters, inducing constant positive energy and good vibes in us. Conversely, negative experiences have tremendous adverse effects on our physical and mental existences. Until we directly face and walk-through that experience or problem related with it, it will always stay with us as a part of us, troubling us. My life experiences say that negative experiences or negativity have more powerful effect on living compare to positive experiences or positivity, especially for those with vulnerable or weak minds.

People suffering from mental health issues such as chronic depression, anxiety disorder, PTSD, schizophrenia or stress and exhibiting physical and mental struggle for survival can agree that our mind is our best friend and our worst enemy. None can do the best and worst to us more efficiently than our own minds, our thought processes and our way of thinking do to us. We're the creators and the killers of our own existences- due to overwhelming capacity and capabilities of our own minds. It takes commitment to self, and persistence, perseverance and resolve to overcome our deepest fears. We must realize that we're the controller of our destiny. We've got in-built divine power and guide to help us alter our fate through our deeds. Hence, we must rise above our fears before they engulf our gullible minds. We don't want our bodies and minds to suffer. So, strong people instead of allowing a long refractory period, walk straight into the trauma or fear and quickly get control over their situations. Thus, that unique experience turns out to be an incredible blessing and learning for them. Learning of life lessons and moving ahead isn't easy, always. It's an emotional and often very painful phenomenon, nonetheless, essential element for a graceful survival and physical and mental health and well-being of a sufferer.

FEAR- can be the root cause of all miseries in life, I believe. Our fears may be related with self-image, fear of- rejection, failure, exams, or fear of losing the battle while trying to win! Fear leads to fright, fright leads to insecurity, insecurity leads to self-doubt, self-doubt leads to loss of confidence and self-control. Self-control is the biggest weapon to protect us against any sort of catastrophe and loss in life, I trust. The moment we lose trust in ourselves and our capabilities, we become physically and mentally weak and fragile. The loss of self-control exposes us and makes us vulnerable, increasing chances of our failure.

The loss of self-control makes us dependable on others for our life choices and actions making us vulnerable in every way. In addition to the physical and emotional challenges, it can have social and mental effects like isolation, stress, depression, or anxiety causing irretrievable damage to us which can destroy us!

It's not your heart, but your MIND, which is competent enough to give you inconceivable troubles while facing challenges related to your mental health - I believe. I agree to the fact that a lot of people's stress, anxiety and/or depression is caused by diverse triggers like constant negative thinking, life losses, loss of hope, failure or fear of failure, feeling of insecurity, persistent niggling feeling of helplessness to achieve something while deprived of something and striving hard to achieve the same. Constant self-dissatisfaction, questioning, or complaining about the purpose and meaning of self-existence, disappointed with own accomplishments, feeling unhappy with everything around or being cynical are typical reasons to slip into severe depression or anxiety syndromes. All of these are typical reasons too why do people vanish from the earth in a blink of eyes! At times, an upbringing shaping a person's thinking pattern may also play a great role. Depression can sometimes surprise us, like a sudden haze rolling in apparently out of nowhere. First timers are generally unaware of its effects and consequences. However, those who are aware and familiar with their personal initial warning signs (may be through their experiences or through others' experiences) can see the first signs of haze sneaking in. Hence, it becomes important to know these signs. If you see this haze approaching you, stop it before it gets too thick and blocks your vision and finally invade your peaceful life.

I do comprehend that hormones, external environment, life choices and life conditions also play great roles. Nevertheless, there is no one size fits all approach when it comes to alleviating the suffering of the sufferer. I do believe, there is a common thread in conditions of many people, though and that is—unhealthy thinking patterns, strong negative approach, denial mode and cynicism. If that is true for you, then being aware of this enables you to gain clarity and understanding about what you are dealing with.

Wake up each day with a smile on your face; fight your demons with strength, grace, and dignity! Wake up with your plan of action to be better than you were yesterday! Wake up to make yourself feel proud and work steadfastly to destroy your inner demons, win over your weaknesses. It's wise to know that medicines may not be an ideal solution for you, if you don't make yourself strong enough to defy the challenges that have put you into this situation.

Through this inspiring and motivating real life story of Dr. Liza, I would love to reach out and help those enduring mental health issue and sufferings wherever I can. I think my book will constructively benefit them to make them able to take steps to regain control of their mental and physical health.

USHA DABAS

(bookauthor@live.com)

CHAPTER 1

It was a regular day of the early March month. It was as usual, a very busy, hectic day at my work. I got very late in the evening to return home. My wristwatch was showing 8.30 pm. when I finished my work. Usually, I accomplish my office tasks latest by 7.00 pm. Today, it took a lot more time. I hit the road hurriedly to go home soon after completing my pending work assignment. I was feeling a lot tired and over-stressed. I was in hurry to go back home and relax.

"This work sucks, it's gonna kill me one day, for sure!" I muttered in dismay while opening the door of my car and started driving in jiffy.

On the way back home, I picked up a box of pizza, two muffins and few Timbits from a nearby Tim Horton outlet for my dinner.

'Not at all my kind of meal, per se'—I agreed with myself.

I truly believe in healthy eating habits. My diet has been always nutritious, and I do prefer home cooked food for my routine breakfast, lunch and dinner. Then why was I eating such junk food! It was a question to ask myself.

At the dinner table, I was pondering over how I my dietary habits had changed in last few months. Not only diet, many of my habits and behavioral pattern have changed altogether. It was not 'ME' anymore. I was a different person in my body, and that strong feeling had affected me from top to the bottom, in and out. How could a life change so radically that I was unable to comprehend!

It was approximately 10.30 pm in my wall clock. I had just completed my daily chores.

Before going to bed, I satisfactorily completed other preparations for the next day's lecture for my students at the college. This was my daily routine. Although I was very tired, I felt happy accomplishing my obligations toward my work. Work is worship, I follow. Academics is the field of my choice, my passion. I have always believed in punctuality and aptness in every task and responsibility I performed.

I had a class scheduled in the next morning at 8.30 am. I meticulously arranged my papers and documents in my folders for the class exams I was going to conduct next morning. Subsequently, I went to bed with my best friend Rocky, my dog, besides me. That night, I was able to fell in to sleep faster than I can ever remember. Generally, I would sleep after 11.00 pm. Today, probably I was too tired to stay awake any longer. Winter was almost at its end in Ontario; nonetheless, the weather was very cold with chilly winds blowing across the streets in Toronto.

In the middle of the night, I got up abruptly in a complete bewilderment and confusion! I was feeling abnormal sensations like burning and electric shock waves running through my body. Initially there was like a general tightening in the legs and feet, but soon, I started getting the same tightening feel around my body.

Next moment, I found myself profusely sweating with incredibly bizarre feelings in my whole body and scary thoughts in my mind. It was for the first time ever in my life that I'd such a frightening experience of getting up in the middle of the night in utter incomprehension without any apparent reason. The feelings I was going through at that time were unable to describe in words! I was still in the bed.

I glanced at the alarm clock beside my bed. It indicated 2:10 am in large orange numbers.

What was that I was feeling about? Was that a very scary dream I saw? Was that a real feeling? I tried to figure out with great efforts. But all in vain. I kept lying in the bed, but was too confused for what to do-keep lying or get up?

I was feeling a terrible headache and temporary loss of vision in both of my eyes. There was a sense of transient paresthesia prevailing in both of my upper and lower extremities. Then, there was an impulsive jerk which shook me entirely and literally pulled me out of my bed. It was so sudden that Rocky, my dog, who was sleeping on his bed besides me also got up and jumped out of his bed in utter confusion. I was absolutely confused and clueless of what was happening to me. There was a sense of terrible unease prevailing in my entire body and mind. I had got a dreadful feeling as if I was losing all control over my body and mind.

At that point of time, I was totally flabbergasted and oblivious to the gravity of the situation. I was unaware of the fact that how much serious the whole matter was going to be soon, not only changing my life, but also my concepts and perspectives towards the life, forever! That time I was purely ignorant to the reality that it was just a tip of an iceberg of my future predicaments.

That was just a beginning of my terrifying phase of emotional crisis of self-identity and composure, I realized soon! The inconceivable experience of that night really changed my awesome life into a nightmarish awfulness; completely shattering my confidence and self-determination in many ways.

I immediately thrown myself out of the bed and rushed downstairs to drink some water in an effort to pacify and revive myself. It proved futile. My bedroom was on first floor. I felt like falling down the stairs as I hurried towards the ground floor of my home. I was unable to remain stable owing to obvious trouble in walking and loss of balance.

My heart was pounding very heavily. I was puffing loudly and gasping for breath. I was experiencing sudden dizziness, numbness, and weakness in my face, hands and feet. I felt like crying loudly. I started slapping my face to feel some sensation as I feared getting paralyzed.

Nearly half an hour passed in this plight and confusion. At this juncture, I was totally bewildered and unmindful at what was going on with my body. I tried to utter a word talking to self but exhibited trouble in speaking. I still had blurred vision in both of my eyes. There was severe, continuous headache with no apparent sickness or health issue. It was all very sudden and unexpected, per se!

I was completely agitated and panicked at that time. I forgot to put the glass of water back on the table after sipping some water from it, which slipped from my hand, fell on the floor and broke down, startling me further. I was unable to regulate my breath and was completely distraught. While taking deep breaths every few minutes, I started moving my hands and legs in the manner to calm down and make myself feel safer and more comfortable – but it made no difference.

I felt a strong wave of trepidation and accelerated heartbeat as soon as I realized the fact that I was all alone by myself. There was no one to help me at home!

At that very point of time, I resolved to call for an emergency help or an ambulance, if my plight continuous further. I contemplated to call 911. I remained sitting on the stairs. I felt as if I was left with no energy to stand up and unable to walk any further. But somehow my inner self was insisting me to fight back the situation with my inner strength. Rocky, my dog was beside me throughout the crisis providing me the invariable emotional support. He was also bewildered and confused, though.

I was fearing for anything and everything-unanticipated and undesirable.

Terrifying thoughts started engulfing my mind with tough questions but no answers—what has happened to me? Am I getting paralysis/paraplegia/hemiplegia? What has the future in store for me? How would I be able to contact anyone if something worst coming next or What if I die?!

My body was getting totally numb and mind was surrounded by delusional thoughts and unforeseen paranoia. I was feeling very anxious and helpless that point of time. I felt like crying loudly. I started frantically pacing around the room and in my hallway in an attempt calm myself. I assumed that pacing movement could reduce my adrenaline levels if they are high and ease the situation.

My imaginations were going berserk. I feared the worst—OMG, maybe I've got my first heart attack! Really?!

"These are all seemingly the signs of first cardiac stroke or heart attack!" my fear was intensified by my own scary thoughts.

There was no warning. I couldn't believe it was coming! There was no prodrome indicating the onset of any disease before specific signs and symptoms could develop. The onset was as sudden as a car crash. Something in my body or brain had gone dramatically and irreversibly wrong, I felt.

My noisy internal monologue—flitting from happiest time of my school days and childhood to present day insecurities—merged around one certain trepidation: 'I'm gonna die... I'm dying. I'm dying'.

I calculated my exact age—so weird! I was 49 years old, precisely. Few days or couple of months more or less won't make any change to my providence, though! I felt more disconcerted and agitated. Nearly an hour and half were spent in pacifying my inner self and recovering from this unanticipated sudden medical emergency. My internal strength was resisting me for seeking any outside help in the form of calling emergency services or 911. My heart was persuading me to remain calm and strong at that crucial hour of crisis.

There was continuous agitation going on between my internal strength and my inner demons, between good side and evil side of mine. It was hard for me to decide who would win! One would make me; another would break me—I realized soon.

'Am I going to break down at this juncture, or would I prove to be strong and determined enough to fight back my demons, full throttle?' I was not sure.

Next moment a comforting certainty came to my mind, that none in my entire family had ever suffered from a small cardiac ailment, leave aside heart attack. All elders of my family- my father, grandfather, grandmother, great grandfather or great grandmother- all had lived and died healthy and happy. Even I was blessed with a very happy and apparently healthy life. As per a healthy lifestyle standard I was availing the benefits of critical health numbers, including weight, blood sugar, BP and cholesterol. I was having all body values and vital signs nearly perfect. I'd always believed and followed a healthy living pattern, comprising of a healthy diet and very conscious life all the way through, with emphasis upon constant upgrading the living standards closely related to quality of life. Everyone was admiring my great physical health and perfect physic until now.

That very thought that I was healthy and physically strong gave me instant relief from evil thoughts pervading my mind. I tried to boost my energies by positive thinking and recapitulating my wonderful life journey till date. Having earned significant level of professional success, high regard, and admiration, I was an achiever at both- personal and professional levels in my life, I recalled. I must reflect on my achievements and successful life, I thought at that very point of time, cheering up my distraught self. I am a medical professional—a successful psychiatrist, and I needed to be strong, always—physically and mentally. I encouraged myself and felt a bit embarrassed for being so weak suddenly, which was against my basic nature.

I don't remember how long I kept sitting on the stairs and when my palpitations subsided. My tremors gradually came down and other symptoms nearly began to fade away. Once I noticed that my symptoms were lessening, I began to breathe slowly and firmly. I was feeling a bit better. I was feeling fatigued and pretty much worn out after the symptoms subsided, though.

After few more minutes, I noticed significant improvement in my condition. I heaved a sigh of relief and went back to the bed in order to get some sleep. It was very late in the night and I was obviously concerned for avoiding any disruption with my next day schedule.

I don't remember exactly what time I fell asleep. Rocky, my companion, slept by my side giving me great support throughout that night. He could sense something was wrong with me. His unconditional love has had always been fulfilling and therapeutic to me. He behaved very responsibly and provided me constant warmth and comfort during that rough night.

Next morning, it was 7.30 a.m. when I woke up! It was really very late by my standards since I'd always be out of my bed by around 5.30 in morning. Whole of my life I practiced 'early to bed, early to rise' discipline, barring the periods of sickness or exceptional conditions. Being successful means waking up early–I was taught in school. Waking up early makes you more productive, healthier, and happier, and you feel in control of your life, I believe. Waking up late was weird and unexpected of me. I felt really very bad, sad, and lost that time.

I got ready in a jiffy leaving behind the dreadful night memories and left for my college. On the way to my college, my mind kept on thinking about the last night's troublesome occurrence. That bad night, unpleasant memory, fresh in my mind was still haunting me. I was worrying about it. I should not pay much attention to it, though, as it did happen just once; I tried to pacify my anxious mind and distressed heart that moment.

Waking up in the middle of the night is pretty much the worst thing, I knew. If that happens every single night when you're just trying to get some restful sleep, it becomes a nightmarish, only the people with such experience in the life, can swear by.

I was worried due to the fear gripping my mind that what if such nightmarish experience turned into every night reality!?

In my younger days, I had seen my best friend's mother suffering from insomnia. She had great difficulty in falling and staying asleep. She was used to spend most nights without a wink. She would wake up often during the night with severe trouble going back to sleep. Now after passing through the hell of my depression and anxiety's dual torments, I can say that I'd been there and can say how does it feel to suffer from insomnia! It's the feeling as if every passing hour presents another challenge to look at the clock and remind yourself just how little sleep you're getting and how appalling you're going to feel come sunrise.

You have your personal, professional, and social commitments too during the day. Not all have means to share their personal troubles and problems with others, though who may empathize with them. So, they keep suffering silently. There are plenty of predicaments naturally associated with the sleeplessness. Having difficulty sleeping can also make anxiety, stress, and depression symptoms worse. However, this was just a single night experience for me that time. So, I didn't ponder much over it, obviously.

Next couple of nights passed rather peacefully. Thankfully, nothing much perceptible or untoward happened. I did not exhibit any considerable health issue as well. I was convincing myself constantly not to ponder much upon about the that fateful night's scary experience and just to discard as an isolated incidence.

Consoling my inner self was much needed at this juncture. My fear and apprehension were not totally subsided, though. Hence, I remained a bit alert every night. I consciously tried to forget the fateful night while putting my brave front forward and haunting incident in the back. I was trying every way for my morale boosting.

How far I succeeded in those unrelenting efforts of my self-encouragement, I realized after few uninterrupted, not-so-bad quality of restful nights.

I could vividly remember that was the frosty morning of March 29th. Few more days and nights had passed amidst myriad of varied feelings after that fateful night of trepidation.

It was a freezing start of the day with heavy snow fall and chilly winds blowing during that morning. I slept late previous night due to extreme workload and stress and continued sleeping until 7.45 am the next morning. When I woke up, I realized that I was going to be late for school. This was not me, per se. I was very late, I realized. I usually started my day early in morning around 5.30 am. Anyway, this had been my new routine attributed to my mental disturbance and sad feelings, and I was excusing me for the self-indiscipline for that reason. I took Rocky, my furry friend out for a walk and then prepared my breakfast in a jiffy. It remained a short walk for Rocky due to time constrain on my part, which he really disliked. He always enjoyed long walks. We returned home in only 15 minutes. There was no time to do anything other than getting a quick shower.

My college was nearly 45 minutes' drive from my home. I was driving cautiously as slow as ever that morning due to slippery ice and snow on the roads. I was expecting a dreadful black ice condition on roads that day, which always feared me a lot.

It was a beginning of the spring season of the year. That day was feeling more like mid-winter day, though. The temperature had plummeted to two digits in minus numbers. The weather was very frigid and unpleasant. Besides, a massive snowstorm was predicted for the southern Ontario region. CBC News in my car radio FM gave latest coverage, "Chilly Arctic air is keeping whole Toronto and GTA area under extreme cold weather warning as icy Arctic air descends on province. The city prepares to tackle the extreme bad weather and snowstorm condition." I was alert. "Toronto is forecast to have extremely cold wind chills on the next two consecutive nights as well". Meteorologist for Environment Canada based in Toronto announced.

"The forecast is calling for a high of −15º C. People are advised to avoid outings in snowstorm prone areas." The headlines in the newspapers also read similar warning that morning.

The city was already geared up to tackle the weather conditions and any adversity associated with the heavy storm damage. It's challenging to drive in such intimidating chilly weather. I was aware of the inclement weather conditions and therefore, was pretty much ready to deal with it.

"The best thing would be, to limit the time outside," I forewarned myself. "The extremely cold weather is unusual this late in winter, and even though it's not unusual to get these kinds of cold snaps. But to get them so late in the winter season is fairly uncommon." I agreed to myself.

I was apprehensive of getting late to college. The very thought made me awfully nervous. I felt uncomfortable and outlandish. I had yet to organize class and study materials for my students of Office Administration. I had to conduct a seminar followed by final exam as well. All that would take considerable time of mine. I must hurry up.

It was 9.45 am. when I arrived at the main gate of my college. I rushed to the front door. There was no one at the front desk. That meant no one saw me coming late! I heaved a sigh of relief and thanked God. Hurriedly, I dashed inside my class.

It was the final exam day for the ongoing batch of Medical Administration class. The students were preparing for their upcoming externship. Their practicum placement was scheduled at the healthcare facilities the upcoming week. It was the final day for their theory class as well. All were excited and gearing up for the professional challenges they'd have to confront soon. I had to discuss with them the strategies to face career related challenges and best possible approaches to tackle them. It was a cheerful atmosphere in the class.

It was freezing outside. Our classroom was near the exit door. The cold was so severe that we were feeling unease even inside the heated room. The door was frequently getting open and closed due to people entering and exiting from it, making our room further cold. The thermostat of the room heater was set at 68 °F, yet it was insufficient to warm us up. I requested my office administrator to increase the room temperature. She acted soon and adjusted the thermostat of room heater at higher temperature. It took some time to achieve increased temperature in the room. After one hour the room was perfectly heated. Initially, I was feeling too cold, but surprisingly, started feeling hot soon after the second time the heater started.

It was 12.35 pm. The students were nearing completion of their test.

Suddenly, I began sweating on forehead and neck regions, and feeling a bit restlessness. In next few minutes, I developed shortness of breath and mild to moderate palpitations. I was in the state of sheer confusion regarding my condition that point of time. I continued deep breaths to revive myself.

Few more minutes passed in dilemma. I continued deep breathing and tried to distract my mind. I was tense and stressed, though. My focus was upon my main task of today. I wanted the exams to get over on time and without any trouble, but the task seemed to be difficult, looking at my condition!

I started feeling sick and woozy. My hands and feet were feeling very cold and numb. I was feeling dizzy. Approximately 20 minutes passed in dilemma of what was happening to me and what should I do in that situation?

Suddenly, I felt like a sharp, shooting, and radiating pain in my chest. Next, I started feeling a terrible headache and everything I saw looked fuzzy and disoriented. It was all sudden. It was more like a dream with no meaning. I tried to get up from my chair but started to feel like swaying, like I couldn't stand straight. The heater kicked in for a third time, and all I remember was very dark minuscule dots covering my eyes and then nothing. Suddenly, the world went wobbly and then I passed out.

The last thing I could remember was-Anita, one of my students, saying something to me, before I fell on the floor, and the very next moment everything went black!

I am not sure how much time elapsed after that. I could just recollect feeling of a sharp, burning pain on my forehead and nose regions when I woke up. There was a small puddle of blood right by my side, on the floor. My nose felt numb yet twitchy. I had hit the chair in front of me on the way down, I was told by my students standing bewildered by my side.

I had yet to regain my full senses. I could indistinctly hear footsteps of people back and forth moving in and out of the hall, and heard one of my fellow teachers saying, "It's ok, you'd just passed out"... It was difficult to comprehend for me anything at that juncture.

I couldn't believe what the people in the room were saying to me. I was like 'passed out'?!... Really...! 'How could I pass out?!'

For me, it was really not done. When something like that happens, especially, in front of a crowd having people known to you, it's embarrassing too!

I kept lying there motionless for a while. My body was hurting me a lot and was feeling nearly senseless. I don't recollect how long I was out there in that situation while constantly feeling lightheaded and disillusioned. Nevertheless, I kept struggling. When I finally woke up, I found myself slumped in a chair. There was a pungent smell of some medicine filling the air surrounding me. My eyes got set on a small group of people standing around me and staring at me in incomprehension.

At first, I was like "Where the heck am I"! I was in the state of bewilderment and confusion. Subsequently, I saw my family doctor, who is also happened to be my good friend, standing next to me, wearing a bit curious and concerned look.

It took me a while to comprehend what had happened to me. I was at my doctor friend's office, the right place for me to be at that very point of time. Since her office was adjacent to my college, my people preferred to rush me there immediately rather than calling 911. I was still like delusional and could only recollect that I was at the college conducting final exams for my students and nothing beyond that.

My doctor heaved a sigh of relief when I looked at her and smiled feebly, since she had contemplated to send me in emergency in a while. She gave me a glass of orange juice and advised to relax for a while. I continued to feel dizzy and nauseous. I kept lying there for nearly an hour or so.

After like, an hour of rest and getting some nutrition, I started feeling a little bit better. Henceforth, I got up and started walking towards my students. Everyone seemed to be a bit relieved to see me back amidst them. I kept struggling to behave as natural and normal as possible. I don't know how far I succeeded in that, though.

I kept smiling at others. I was not a one bit alright, nonetheless, inside. I'd realized, I had some "issue" with me!

In a short while, my doctor took me inside her room to discuss my condition. She asked me few questions pertaining to my daily life, routine, and relations. She asked me whether I was as happy as the others around me. Did I feel any unusual development in my life quite recently? She also enquired whether I felt fearful for no reason or tend to focus on upsetting situations or events happening in my life. She asked me few more questions regarding my personal life, any traumatic past experience etc. etc. to which I replied as per my comprehension at that time.

She finally concluded by describing my current situation as "Panic attack" as the manifestation of something related to my mental condition, I might be going through.

The information, in true sense panicked me! The very term 'Panic Attack'- literally panicked me! I was least prepared to hear that. It totally freaked me out! It's really terrifying to hear such thing. However, it's more significant, when the patient with mental health issue is a Psychiatrist!

Panic Attack and Me! It was an ill-fitting combination. It wasn't logical too for the person normally having high morals and great level of self-confidence. That revelation instantaneously sent chills down my spine!

A whole lot of scary feelings attacked my body. Frankly, the very thought of having panic attack or mental health issue was downright frightening! My blood ran cold, it scared me so much. I felt numbness throughout my body and my brain lost the thinking power! I was yet not ready to accept the reality; I was on totally denial mode. I'd had a rocky road with mental health; this was difficult to digest for me.

I started coughing and fidgeting. I was feeling agitated at that point of time. Seeing upon me getting freaked out, my doctor advised me to calm down and relax. She offered me a glass of water. She left the room after some time. I was alone in a room for a while. My mind started pondering over what my doctor had apprised me of a short while ago.

After a deliberate thinking for 10-15 minutes, I started realizing the element of truth in her statements. I realized what I'd been suffering with was a considerable problem with anxiety for couple of months now. The fact that my life had always seemed to be perfect and yet I was experiencing such terrible things— that paradox of my life was inconceivable for me. It instantaneously made me feel vulnerable and powerless.

I kept sitting there my head holding in my hand, engulfed in deep thought processes. My mind was inundated with the thoughts and feelings of anguish, disagreement, embarrassment, and disbelief. There were a lot of confusion and a lot of perplexity.

My doctor returned to me after some time. She asked me how I was feeling. She advised me to go home and take rest. She also prescribed me some sedatives in case I might need to sleep restfully that night.

I kept seating in the chair in the doctor's office for some more time and returned to my class a bit confounded and a bit indecisive. Everyone kept staring at me askance and with sort of sympathy towards my plight. Some of them were looking at me dubiously rather than thoughtfully, I felt. It was very hard for me to face those stares. I was literally working hard to avoid those mixed feelings' gazes.

It was really funny that some total strangers present there were also asking me how I was feeling... how embarrassing! But that was not all, I was feeling like I'd lost my confidence, my power, my vigor and vitality. It was my inner struggle I was actually fighting with and was troubling me at that very point.

'What has happened to me? Am I getting abnormal!?? Is this the repeat of my previous night's bad experience? Will that keep repeating? What is wrong with me! Am I getting Mad?!' My mind was constantly struggling to find out the answers to those questions.

I gathered my leftover strength and resumed my work. Each passing moment was agonizing. Remaining day was nothing but an unsought torture. I somehow managed to complete my class and returned home with my mind going berserk full of apprehension and bewilderment.

After that unanticipated incident, the rest of the day remained a big disaster for me.

That day was the first day to mark perhaps the beginning of my predicaments, I can say so now.

◆ ◆ ◆

At home, I was by myself, all alone. Being alone doesn't mean lonely; I always argued with people who had confusion about their meanings and used them interchangeably. I'd had stayed alone for many months, probably couple of years in different countries while I was on my professional assignments. Nonetheless, I never felt bad about solitude. I never felt lonely; typically, some people may feel in that condition. On the contrary, I enjoyed being alone at times, while relishing me-time and utilizing my 'alone' time as a best opportunity for self-development.

It was a different story this time, however. This time I was alone but, I was lonely too.

Probably, I was lonelier, I confessed to myself. I wished my family to be by my side this time! I wanted from the bottom of my heart to share my feelings-good and bad-with someone close to me. But there was no such luck!

All in the neighborhood were indoors all through day and night, to avoid cold in this extreme winter weather. The streets were deserted most of the time. I was like dying to see someone. I was so keen to talk with someone, anyone, with whom I can share talk of a humdrum routine work, even if not any specific one. But it was hard luck for me. No one happened to be around. Days and nights were passing just like that. Everywhere it was like an atmosphere of gloom, dejection and apathy was prevailing, sure enough to induce instant depression and anxiety even in a normal person!

I was feeling like crying aloud to grab attention of someone. It had been a couple of months since I'd a word with anyone in the neighborhood, I recollected, while unlocking my front door.

'How the people in modern times are confined to themselves? No one is bothered about good or bad of others' life. No one cares, even if you die in this depressing, extreme cold weather!' I talked to myself with a deep sigh.

With a heavy heart, I entered inside my home. I realized soon with deep anguish—I was returning to an empty house, same one, which I left in the morning. I was doing same every day. It was not only empty house. I was feeling empty inside too.

Everything inside the house was silent except Rocky, my dog-very energetic, ever happy-go-lucky one. Upon seeing me back from the work, as usual he became super excited and insanely happy. Soon he jumped over me and crazily started licking me all over my face. He did expect my typical happy response in the return, which was missing today, though. Had it been any other day, I could have certainly joined him in his crazy expression of eternal love and happiness. I used to pet him, caress him, hug and kiss him. We both would run wildly all over the house.

Today, the things were totally different. I was sad and dejected. Life, it seemed, as if was thrown out of the gear. Everything was nothing but gloom and dejection for me at that time. I'd never felt so miserable and lonely before.

I took a deep sigh. My mind was obviously lost in deep thoughts. An eerie silence was prevailing everywhere inside my house. Straightaway, I climbed the stairs to reach my bedroom. Rocky kept watching me sadly. My head was aching terribly. I was feeling like going to sleep right away.

I realized soon that Robin, my youngest son, wouldn't be in his room, where usually he used to be during that time of the day, until a couple of months ago. But not now. He'd also left for another country few days ago. His two elder siblings had already left home earlier to follow their dreams. As a mother, I loved all my children but, being youngest, Robin was dearest of all.

Like his elder siblings, Robin too had plans for his life. He wasn't interested to walk on the career path his parents had suggested to him, which they believed would provide him a successful professional career.

I and my husband had vast knowledge and experience in diverse fields of education, and we were willing to guide him. I wished he should stay with me at least for few years. That turned out to be my thinking, though. I could have been a great support for all his career and life decisions, I'd perceived. However, he wasn't interested in my guidance. His notion and ways about living his life were different from that of mine. He'd decided to walk on his path on his own. I should not be meddling with his life and life plans, I realized. I'd held back myself, remembering the mistakes I'd made before, which often led to unsavory arguments and debates between us. Finally, I'd respected his decision. He was happy with his decision, and so was I.

I felt as if I was awfully missing him, though. With moist eyes, I looked at the closed doors of his room. I wished against the certainty that he could be there and wish me a soft 'hello'. Even if he doesn't add pronoun 'Mom' with his 'hello' I would not mind, my aching heart conversed with my troubled mind. In true love, you can tolerate some indiscipline.

Tears fell down my cheeks.

"Are you missing him?" My heart questioned me inquisitively.

"Of course, I do", I agreed, "This's the very attribute of being a mother." I told my aching heart. I walked past his room with a heavy heart and moist eyes.

Missing him wasn't the only issue. As a matter of fact, I was worried about his wellbeing too. He would be by himself, all alone, in an unfamiliar place. How would he manage his living and life? He didn't even bother to call me back, though, while I was overly concerned about him. I felt saddened. But that's the life! Probably, I was overly interfering in his personal matters.

"He's a grown-up boy, he can manage" I consoled my aching heart and wiped my moist eyes.

Whole evening my heart kept aching. Due to heart, we have feelings and those feeling at times put us in trouble, especially when we become exceedingly sentimental. There were abundance of anguishes and pains created by that aching heart. I'd plentiful of problems of my own, I must live my life, I can't live life of others. Now, I was required to gear up for something very crucial, very decisive, of course, against my heart, my extreme emotions, I told myself.

Next stage for me was to get ready for tough love! Tough love for myself—I felt probably I was overly pampering my emotions. I wanted to restrain my benevolence to my aching heart, which was creating problems for me. I was needed to be very strong, so that I can help myself solve my own problems. There was a battle going on between my emotions and my practicality.

Needless to mention, that night was full of nightmares. My mind was bursting with agonizing thoughts and unpleasant feelings. The whole night I just kept waiting for the dawn to break.

Next afternoon, I visited my family physician in her office. I told her about my previous day's happening. She checked me and asked some basic questions such as how I was feeling, whether I was able to sleep well previous night, and based upon her examination she decided to keep me under observation. She preferred not to refer me for consultation to any specialist for the time being.

"You're just feeling tired and exhausted due to over work, my dear," my doctor opined. "Have good food and good sleep, and you would be just fine." She stated.

I was diagnosed as a normal but overworked individual needing rest and discharged after the routine medical assessment. Somehow, that was what I wanted perhaps at that point of time. To be honest, I was a bit against making my situation open to people. I didn't want to expose my weakness any further to anyone, known or unknown. I agreed at once to the proposal of keeping me under observation.

Meanwhile, my doctor went on her vacation for nearly 15 days.

I continued feeling awful subsequent days too. Consequently, I decided to check with the doctor after a week's time. My feelings were gradually turning bad to terrible. Another physician at the same medical office examined me that time. Similar opinion of my overworked and overstressed condition was expressed by him after checking me. He advised me to follow up with him after a week to decide about the further course of the treatment or referral to a specialist if the need arose. My family physician was still on vacation.

I was back to square one with all the guesses about my situation. My real health issue remained veiled under those assumptions and presumptions.

I was not in proper shape of mind, slowly but surely, I was arriving to the understanding. I may be going to have tough time experiencing sleepless nights now on, I feared drastically amid inexplicable drama and confusion. I kept avoiding any medication (the doctor who checked me last time prescribed me sedatives in case I need to take) throughout this time, though.

A week passed with ingrained emotional upheavals. At times, I feared too much about unforeseen things. Often, I would get hallucinations. I was unsure about my own actions and unconfident about my abilities. I was determined to avoid any sort of therapy at that juncture simply to prove myself.

CHAPTER 2

LATE APRIL 2015

Going to work every morning was a challenge for me since I had to constantly wear a mask of my usual self, the way people knew me—a strong, erudite, and competent professor. On the contrary, under that mask, I was totally a weak, broken, directionless individual with lost confidence. My inner strength was fighting at full throttle with my weaknesses, my hidden demons, though. Thankfully, no one knew about my sad fact.

Meanwhile, I kept avoiding any major socialization or attending any meeting, party or public gathering to avoid major interactions with people. I was not confident enough for different kinds of public dealings. At times, I would feel a bit easy in isolation, but for a short time. Soon after finding me alone, my demons started haunting me. Everyone, including my family and friends had deserted me, no one cared for me, I would die dreadful death in isolation soon—those feelings were growing stronger within me, each passing day.

I could vividly remember the mornings, evenings, and nights when I used to constantly stare at my clock counting seconds and minutes to reckon with the passing time. It was terrifying to count and match every gone hour with remaining hours in the day! How weird it was that I felt relieved by knowing only few hours were left in the day and new day would begin, with the hope that it would bring some respite in my condition! The thought of being deserted would fill my mind with uncanny horror feelings.

Few more days passed in this dilemma of what to do and what to avoid as a preventive measure and maintain status-quo.

Eventually after few days, one of my doctors advised me to go for medications. The decision to take some anti-anxiety pills came after assessing my condition for few more days. He suggested me a high dose of medication. Nonetheless, that was not the cure of my condition, but to have a peaceful sleep at night. What I truly needed was a good nigh sleep. The sleep was eluding me like forever, I agreed.

I preferred to experiment with mild medications initially, though. Hence, the doctor changed his prescription to oral pills of sedatives- Zopiclone-1 O.D. (once at bedtime). I knew Zopiclone belongs to class of medications called sedative-hypnotics. I prescribed them in the past for my patients in my clinical practice for short-term and symptomatic relief of sleep disturbances. I felt Zopiclone could help me with my conditions of difficulty falling asleep, frequent wakeups during night and early morning awakenings. I was concerned for side effects, though. It might induce daytime drowsiness, dizziness and lightheadedness.

My concern was that I was working during day and the medication may create problem for me. I was also a bit sceptic about the benefit or suitability of the medicine for me. 'What if I still continue with the existing predicaments?' fear was looming large.

After much of deliberation and contemplation, I took a single tablet that night and waited for its effect. The pill worked. I was able to sleep. I would not say it peaceful or deep sleep category, but it was like ok, better with it than without it. However, I decided not to continue for any further since I started feeling a bit weird after taking the medicine. I was like nauseous and dizzy during the daytime.

I stopped medication. I trust natural immunity, per se. By and large, I avoid taking medication.

I was clueless how to tackle my issues, now. My doctors were either. They kept insisting on their 'overworked and tired' theory and advised me rest. I was failed to understand what my issues were or how actually all started in first place.

Few more days passed. The days were dreadful, but nights were terribly agonizing. Scary nightmares became regular features. The bouts of anxiety kept haunting me continuously. There were constant niggling voices running in my head. My cognizance was doubting everything I did, and the actions of mine as well as of others. My anxiety was promoting catastrophic thinking in my mind. Doom-and-gloom fantasies were permeating my day while reaching a fever pitch at night when I would be lying in the bed. Those catastrophic visualizations and feelings were not certainly unreasonable, though. Anything could happen; I was convinced inside my heart.

My anxious mind, burdened with far too much free time in the wee hours of the morning would start agonizing over anything- trivial or significant, just anything. It would target some dire, worst-case scenario-predominantly on the subjects of— personal life, relations, finances, health, future, animal cruelty, universe, apocalypse and environment protections or any other topic of the worldly matters. However, those creepy thoughts were gripping my mind in a way that did accomplish nothing other than making me feel miserable and powerless!

At times, my hallucinations and delusional fantasies would be at peak, making me feel scream at highest pitch for help. Few more days and nights passed in those predicament and agonies.

Panic attacks at smallest instance became a regular affair, next. I was putting my brave front and moving forward. Slightest things such as dish slipping from my hand, someone knocking the door, phone ringing, someone calling me when I was engrossed in my work would make me terrified. I would freak out at even negligible occurrences. I felt like crying loudly and relieve myself every now and then.

My only companion, Rocky, was observing me throughout that period of my plight and was trying his best to make me happy and cheerful by his diverse actions.

I've had always believed in privacy of personal matters. Being an introvert person, generally I avoid discussing my own life with anyone.

I was very much confused and unsure about my own condition and feeling a lot nervous that time. Probably, I could have shared my plight with someone who could have empathized with me. Nonetheless, there was no one around me to confine and discuss my problem with - that was hurting me a lot! I felt like ending my life at one point of time, but my morality and ethics reprimanded me, and I pulled through the undignified way to end my miseries.

CHAPTER 3

JUNE 2015

My life had got atrociously changed after that first incident of frightening night in the month of early March. It had been a couple of months now. It was like I was going through a hell.

Too often, I would hear the inconsequential voices in my ears. My mind was constantly occupied with negative thoughts and dreaded notions. I would come home from work and feel so exhausted from all of the voices in my head and negative thought processes that I would prefer to just sleep to block it all out. I didn't want to wake up because living had become like a nightmare. Nevertheless, majority of times sleep would fail to bring much respite to me. I started feeling sick with the fear of nighttime as well since that time the voices got even louder, and my fears got much stronger. I would get so much frustrated because it seemed impossible to sleep, as if my insomnia and my despair were going hand in hand.

I will never forget the fateful day of 8th June. It was one of the worst days of my life!

I was walking my dog in a nearby park in that late afternoon. Generally, I used to take him out for his regular walks twice in a day-once in the morning and once in the evening. However, these days I'd made significant changes to my routine. Whenever possible, we would go for a walk during daytime, at least before evenings and anytime in mornings. I was avoiding dusk and gloom at any cost. I was fearing darkness and loneliness. If there were less people in the streets and less traffic on roads, that was enough to make me feel like haunted and insecure.

While returning home after about an hour walk that afternoon, I took a shorter way to my home than usual longer one to make it to home earliest possible. While walking down the familiar streets, I entered in a lane little less known to me. I kept walking to figure out the exact location, but in vain. I was feeling strange. The lane seemed to be deserted, with no one in the vicinity. I started feeling intimidated due to being in an unknown place.

In a while, I developed the feeling that I had lost my way back home. Subsequently, I became so anxious I couldn't breathe!

Two days ago, I'd read an article about a man in his 40s, in BC province of Canada, lost his way back to his home while returning from work, who was later helped by 911 team to reach home safely. It happened to an apparently a healthy-looking man, who was later diagnosed to be in the early stage of Alzheimer disease.

Could that be me?!!

The very thought of myself getting affected by dementia or Alzheimer increased my palpitation. I began recollecting the recent and near past events of my life and problems in a jiffy, and corelating with the signs and symptoms of dementia and Alzheimer. Ironically, they all started perfectly fitting in the same framework created by my mind!

'Probable Alzheimer'—my mind instantaneously self-diagnosed my condition like an expert neurologist!

Very next moment, I started profusely sweating. I was staring at various street signs, reading names of the streets, pathetically lost in the middle of the road. What happened to me? Am I also suffering from dementia? Alzheimer? Would I die soon? I was so much worried that how will I be able to go home if I get lost, what will happen to my dog and what if I don't remember my home address? Top of all, I felt I have like forgotten my home address!

I tried to recollect the same with added confusion and perplexity, but in vain. I felt like screaming and crying loudly to get help from someone. The street was deserted at that point of time, so, apparently none was available to help me out of my plight. Subsequently, I started contemplating to call 911 and what to tell them, if I got totally lost and fail to find out my way back home on my own? There were too many questions, whats, ifs and buts!

My situation took a turn for the worst, soon. My worst fear came true the very next moment. I was not carrying my cell phone with me, I realized soon with chill running down my spine! I felt like crazy. How could I forget to carry my cell with me, when I was aware that I could be in the situation needing some one's help! I was certainly in disturbed mental state, I realized. The feeling that I was going "mental" was getting more and more horrific and overwhelming for me.

I don't remember how long I kept walking with my dog by my side in sheer state of confusion and trepidation yet pretending to be an absolutely normal person. I also don't remember how much time passed in that state of distress and disorientation.

I was clueless how exactly that happened, but after a while I found myself collapsed by the side of a parked vehicle in an open space nearby the colony park. Upon opening my eyes, I could see someone leaning over me and uttering something to me. I was having no idea what was going on there! A terrible headache was gripping my head, so I kept lying there for a while.

Next, I overheard a man and a woman chatting with each other apparently regarding me and my condition. They were narrating how while walking down the street they saw me wandering in a confused state and immediately rushed to me to help when I suddenly fell to the ground after colliding with a parked truck. They were about to call 911.

I couldn't believe it, I wanted to cry, it was difficult for me to hold myself! Last few months I was struggling with my condition. But I was like 'this would be over soon. It'd be over in a minute, once I will be strong', I was constantly reminding myself each day while fighting with my demons. However, what I really didn't think that it would even go up to an extent that I could lose my control over myself!

That was terrible. That was simply incredible and far-fetched. I felt so much embarrassed about my situation and everything about me at that very point of time. However, it was not the right time to ponder upon the past developments or future. I was needed to take the control of my situation, right now, even if as a temporary measure. Subsequently, I pretended as if I felt a bit dizzy and exhausted while walking due to hot and humid weather to disguise what was really going on with me.

I was in no state to meet eyes with the people who came to help me, but anyway, profusely thanked all the people who gathered there for their kindness and generosity.

With the state of total disillusion and feelings mixed with shame, guilt, and insecurity, I reached home that afternoon.

Little did I know that after that fateful incident, I'd have to continue to mask similar feelings of anxiety for the next many more days and months. Really, one just can't tell by looking at someone how they're feeling inside.

Two days later, I attended a wonderful wedding party of a relative's daughter with my closest family and friends. As usual, I pretended to be a normal person, singing, dancing and rejoicing with the other partygoers while carrying a whole lot of agonies, pain and apprehensions inside me. I'm not really sure about their memory of me that day, since I'd tried to acquire an art of faking by then, however, my only memory of that day was my unceasing thinking that my wonderful professional career was over at the age of 49 because I'd gone "mental"!

Next couple of days, intermittently the same type of phenomena of getting confused or being lost on the way home or while going to work kept happening, compounding my mental health status and creating further dubiety over my self-control and confidence. I behaved in same manner, pretending to be alright, for the following days in similar circumstances. I was unsure and totally oblivious to what was coming my way. It was a dreadful fact, which I was oblivious to, that I'd have to continue to mask my constant feelings of anxiety for the next few more months.

'Never ever go over the looks, the looks may be deceptive' I'd read somewhere. Really, it is impossible to read or judge someone's mind by simply looking at them. An apparently calm and composed looking individual may be undergoing turbulent waves of scary thought processes inside their minds, just crying aloud for the help for the graceful survival. Most likely this cry remains incomprehensible to those who have never gone through such experiences. Seemingly, I was a perfect and normal individual to everyone from outside. They were oblivious to the turbulent rage of ravaging thoughts prevailing inside my mind, though.

The common anxiety symptoms such as having difficulty controlling worry, anticipating negative events and outcomes in almost every task I carried out and having a sense of impending doom—all those things plagued me. I was still clueless and wondering that what had happened to me making me reluctant to get professional help!

My nervousness was a silent force that had literally sabotaged a lot of joy of my everyday life. It held me back from so many things I ever loved to do and enjoyed doing a lot. Small pleasures of life were eluding me.

Amidst all my miseries, two things I found persistent- One was good, another, bad. First one was the weirdest yet solacing that until now no one was able to distinguish any different 'ME' while I interacted with them. And second, my constant fear that I would suffer from severe nervous outbreaks to the point that I would be unable to socialize or perform, had come true and made me difficult to complete my everyday tasks, put aside any new work project!

CHAPTER 4

JULY 2015

I was suffering from- Depression and Anxiety disorder-both at the same time. Finally, I got my diagnosis for my mental health condition.

The news was not like totally unanticipated or out of the blue. There was nothing new and definitely not to feel relieved or be happy about. It was just a matter of finally arriving at a pronouncement of a sick condition, per se. Nonetheless, it was not a solution or remedy for my imminent condition. I was more concerned and worried, however, about- what next? Arriving at a diagnosis was like a verdict given in a long pending criminal case, where the actual sentence was still awaited!

'Having anxiety and depression both at the same time, is not very uncommon', my doctor told me. Revelation of the diagnosis took some time in my case, though. Since there was a great denial from my side to accept the fact that a strong-willed person such as me could suffer from a psychological disorder. Depression or Anxiety and me??! I could never fathom and agree to such an acrid reality. That was not even a distant possibility, in my thinking. I may suffer some psychiatric condition and seek professional help that I could never think in my wildest dream! But unfortunately, that was the truth, and I was required to accept that grim reality.

I knew that the coexistence of anxiety and depression-called comorbidity-as discussed in psychiatry and psychology fields carry some serious repercussions. It makes the course of disorder more chronic; it impairs functioning at work and in relationships more. It also substantially raises suicide risk. I taught the same knowledge to my students in psychiatry classes until a couple years ago.

Depression and anxiety ain't two disorders that coexist, I read in one of the latest medical journals. Both are two faces of one disorder; in the recent times clinicians and researchers have been moving towards theories with more insight into the disorders, the article read further. I was aware that a person who primarily suffers from anxiety is used to focus on future prospects and become overwhelmed with fear that everything will turn out badly—only, this time it was me!

My fear, my dread, my terror feelings, my loss of confidence were restricting my ability to work, maintain relationships or activities in and out of my house. Nowadays, most of the time, I was synthetically comfortable at work, but terrifically disturbed and anxious while being at home. I was pretending to be normal, which I was not one bit, but wanted to save myself from any disaster or accident while being cautious that no one comes to know about my real situation. There was a constant fierce battle going on between myself and my inner demons.

What I was living, I realized soon, was a terribly fake life with loss of self-control under constant fear of losing myself to my inner demons. It was different me during the day and totally opposite by the night. Whole nights I kept waiting for the dawn, which often failed to bring much respite to me. I would keep tossing and turning my sides in the bed throughout night. The constant struggle within was killing me day by day.

A couple years back, in my psychiatry class when I was teaching my students about the anxiety and depression disorders, their causes, and the plight of those suffering from these conditions; I had a least inkling that I'd be at the exact spot in near future! It was too much too soon, though, I guess. During the discussion, I always insisted that those suffering from such demons destroying mental health require crucial help from others. How can the troubled life of those suffering from these demons could be put back on track by helping them live a happy, healthy life, I discussed with intense energy with my students.

How strange it was! I'd forgotten that I was a Psychiatry professor! The biological "fight or flight" response, exhibiting that one's body and mind is often alert and tense, and which is so exhausting and frustrating—now my mind was experiencing. It was my turn now. I was struggling with all those demons! I was talking to myself the same way as I was talking with my students, trying to convince myself that all would be good eventually. It was the time to follow my own advises. The life seemed to have come a full circle, indeed.

Both anxiety and depression were negatively impacting my sleep, routine, and health. I was impacted by bouts of severe anxiety and constant trepidation so much so that I could experience overwhelming fear and panic, similar to any creature fighting for its life in the wild. At times when no one was around me, I would relieve myself by crying loudly. It was the cry for help, cry to make myself free from cruel clutches of unseen demons hiding inside my mind, the demons, perhaps only created by me.

The life was seemingly lusterless, meaningless and hopeless. Often, I used to get engulfed in weird, negative thoughts. The deep-seated issues kept coming on surface, constantly haunting, overwhelming and distracting me from my work and sleep. In the middle of the night, I'd wake up with sleep nowhere in sight for hours together with my mind surrounded by strange and recurring thoughts of committing suicide to end my miseries forever. Was that the perfect answer for all my miseries to end; I wondered, I was not sure, though.

Thankfully, no one around me was suspecting anything unusual about me-behavior wise or performance wise, so far, despite a great war going on inside my mind. My behavior was perfectly normal for others. For them I was my regular self, just a bit tired or busy, if any behavior of mine seemed abnormal to them, if at all. It was a great respite for me, for sure.

It was a trying time for me, and I was constantly struggling to be as normal as possible.

CHAPTER 5

LATER IN JULY 2015

One morning, when I got up from the bed, I was feeling dizzy and confused. I was feeling sick, nauseous and depressed. My anxiety level was at peak. I was very much worried about the preparation for the office meeting I was going to attend that day.

As I started getting ready for the work, I started feeling palpitations. My vision started getting blurred. I felt as if I had a memory loss. I was unable to recollect what I wore the previous day. Even I failed to recollect what office tasks I completed in last two days. My repeated attempts to recollect few things I did on previous day failed too. I was like lost in oblivion. I was freaked out to take in that I'd lost my memory. I just managed to do my things during the day at work. However, my feeling of memory loss got stronger as the day passed.

Late that afternoon, one of my colleagues called me to inquire about the task which I'd to complete 2 weeks ago. I realized I'd failed to do that. I forgot it totally! On the contrary, I asked the caller what it was for, only to get response filled with surprise from him like "Really!!, is that you?!" It was like none could expect such a sloppy attitude from a responsible person like me!

I profusely apologized for my mistake. "No worry. It wasn't urgent. I will do the needful." The fellow took the matter lightly. The matter got resolved amicably. Nonetheless, I felt ashamed of myself for being irresponsible and careless on my part. It would have never happened few months or a couple years ago, I was sure. I believe in commitments. Promises should not be broken, and professional commitments must be fulfilled on timely basis, I profess. Failing at the duty made me feel like awful and reduced my own credibility in my mind instantaneously.

I was going down day by day. My mind was always busy fearing worst all the time. In every little thing, my mind was looking for negativity. Even in most positive and cheerful environment, my mind would find distraught and excuse to be sad and gloomy. Too frequently, I was getting suicidal thoughts. Life was nothing but gloom, pessimism and dejection everywhere.

I recollected someone known to me suffered from anxiety disorder and severe depression many years back. I had his contact number. So curiously and expecting to avail some guidance from him to combat my prevailing condition, I called him one evening. I expected some resourceful information and positive response from his side. After casual formalities exchange, I asked him about his experience at the time of his suffering and how was he doing now. To my utter dismay and shock, he told me that he still gets frequent bouts of anxiety and undergoes moderate to severe depression under certain situations. He narrated how those demons of anxiety and depression kept haunting him and sneaked inside his otherwise normal life, causing nightmares.

"Once you suffer from anxiety and depression, you can never ever get out of them. They become the part of your life. You're compelled to live with the sad fact that you ain't normal, your life isn't normal." His words scared me to death, to be honest!

A person could never be out of anxiety and depression problems, that was the last thing on my mind! It was difficult to digest that one can't come out of that quagmire of negativity, sadness and destruction, however hard one may try! I was disappointed.

I really felt miserable after learning the distressful fact from him that he was not fully recovered from his condition as I'd presumed before I talked with him. That night was horrible for me. I got deliriums and nightmares. Would I be never out of the clutches of these demons called depression and anxiety? The very thought was killing me. I just kept waiting for the dawn to break on a new day.

It's normal to occasionally open your eyes in the middle of the night, glance at the clock and drift back to sleep. However, it becomes a matter of genuine concern when same happens for many days, and it becomes a matter of serious concern when you wake up and stay up, night after night. If this starts happening, believe you need a help. Self-help is the best, still you may need a help from others. If this keeps continuing, some help is needed not to cure only insomnia but to find out the root cause of that happening. Sooner is better. I realized the fact soon.

I'd started losing my sleep progressively. I could sleep only 4-6 hours every night. Getting up from a deep sleep in the middle of the night, mostly around 2 or 3 am and keep awake until alarm rings at 6.00 am became a regular affair. Lack of sleep disturbed my whole routine and badly affected my work. Anxiety disorder had totally changed me from inside. It was a constant vicious war between my inner self and external existence. No one was aware of my inner struggle, though. For me having an anxiety disorder meant that I was losing the sense of my feelings, but I had feelings about my actual feelings, awareness and acceptance of my condition.

I was constantly worried that my feelings weren't real or that my feelings about my feelings are the correct feelings, or my feelings are the wrong feelings. I had all that- shame about my feelings, guilt about my feelings, anger about my feelings, and insecurity about my feelings. Sometimes I even wondered which feeling was real – the initial feeling or the resulting feeling?

Was I making myself feel this way or did I just feel this way? If I am not sure about my feelings, how could I get help from others? I've had been fine all through these years. But now, I had nightmares every night and could barely function at work. "What's going on?" It was a troublesome, yet important question for me.

I started recapitulating last few years' events of my life. I just wanted to check back if anything went wrong or suspicious in my life enough to relate with or blame for my prevailing situation. I was wondering how my whole joyful and contented life had upturned, how my happy routine was thrown out of gear into the state of confusion, disorder, and disarray due to my psychologic status. All my old memories started resurfacing on my mind arena. I'd those repressed memories that were blocked from conscious perception as a result of significant stress. Due to experience of a significant degree of stress or trauma, my sympathetic nervous system had become hyperactivated and overwhelmed my brain, I realized as a medical professional.

"Was that my old, bad memories dumped in some corner of mind coming back to frighten me!? I feel like I'm falling apart, does this mean I'm getting worse each day?" I kept asking myself without any comforting reply.

I was amazed at the fact that how silently and how many demons I was fighting concomitantly putting brave front!

CHAPTER 6

I wasn't keeping well and wasn't happy either due to physical problems. My hormones were fluctuating. I wasn't sure if I was in perimenopausal stage. My periods were getting irregular, scanty and painful and sometimes exhibited menorrhagia. I'd lots of mood swings and xenophobia (strange fear of unknown).

For more than a year, I was suffering from my throat related health issues. I'd been diagnosed with a substantial size laryngeal cyst. Initially, it was a small lump causing mild to moderate discomfort and pain but there was a noticeable increase in its dimension with the passage of time. That had led to constant pain in my throat and significant discomfort and restlessness during speech and swallowing. The problem used to aggravate with cold weather effects leading to severe pain in my throat while talking and left me with coarse voice. I was unable to talk for longer than 20-25 minutes at a stretch.

My throat was dry all the time and the roughness and coarseness of my voice were apparent to the listeners. That had led to considerable problems in conducting lectures for me. Teaching was not only my profession but was my passion and potion- the divine soup for my soul, I believed. I've had always lived my profession of psychiatry and medicine. Teaching, tutoring and touching lives of my students- that's what I ever wanted to do. My students were my family, and my teaching was my life.

My physical condition was hampering my connection with my family, disturbing my life.

Both physical and mental pains were agonizing and worsening day after day. Moreover, I was unable to sing due to my laryngeal cyst lesion. The pain of being unable to sing was much more than being unable to speak for me, since I was a born singer, and I was singing for my soul. My singing was the biggest factor in keeping me alive and fresh all the time. Although, the singing was not my profession, it was my tonic without which I couldn't survive. The pain of losing my voice was agonizing, which could only be understood by a singer who had ever been in the plight of losing their voice.

'Your cystic lesion will require surgical excision if it doesn't get healed in timely manner or if the symptoms get worse', my doctor had pronounced after checking my condition few times in past couple of months. She had scheduled my next consultation with an ENT specialist. I was living in the constant fear of throat cancer, big surgical procedures and may be losing my voice forever! The thoughts were very scary.

Being a teacher, I was compelled to persistently conduct lectures for almost 8-9 hours in a day. I was overusing my vocal cord, per se—a generic attribute of my profession, may be. Yes, that was really an extraordinary burden I was putting on my body. Every job has its own occupational hazards. This was mine. This was–absolutely my occupational health hazard, I had to agree, but was I paying price for being in this noble profession? I just wondered. Having said that, I had to admit there was really a no way out for me. I was required to work that many long hours. It was not possible always that I would get my desired work, in first place. At times, I was out of work for many days and may be a month or two, which was definitely a more devastating factor for me. Hence, at times, I preferred to work for 12-13 hours in a day, since there was no surety of the work very next day! The continuous cold weather was contributing to my plight.

I was under observation by my family doctor and ENT surgeon. ENT surgeon did my check up, prescribed few medications and advised surgery in the event of lesion increased in size or became more progressive. I was praying God and waiting for my cyst to get healed on its own.

Throat issue wasn't only health issue at that time. For last year and half, my nails had gotten brittle and were breaking easily. As a health professional, I knew that nails could reveal clues to our overall health. A touch of white here, a rosy tinge there, or some rippling or bumps-all were sign of something untoward or some disorder in my body. What if there was some problem in my liver, lungs, or heart (which can show up in our nails)! I was feeling terrible. The condition of my nails was probably revealing deep secrets about my health. I was highly worried.

I had a big issue with my hair too. In last more than a year, my hair strength has almost reduced to a half. My hair already had got thinner and hair fall was getting worse day by day. I'd a faded, washed-out look, and my hair was thinning out. I was compelled to cut them off often to maintain the pleasant look and esthetic appeal. It was again painful to see how my lustrous, shiny, black hair had lost their eternal charm and had become lusterless. Nearly one third of them had turned grey too which I was maintaining by coloring them regularly. I was extremely worried for their fate. I was fearing I might go bald soon and ugly looking. It was so scary to imagine such providence and future eventualities!

All things were leading to one direction in life-NEGATIVITY! I had a horrid feeling of like getting failed everywhere, whatever I did or tried to achieve. Few days back, I got failed 6th time in my driving tests, which was unbelievably outrageous! I was too shocked to react to that since I had track record of above

25 years of successful driving. I had spent lots of money, time and energy in preparing myself to get that license in past three years. All remained futile! I got severe depression and anxiety subsequent to failure this time.

CHAPTER 7

AUGUST 2015

I was doing two jobs. I was feeling too much lethargic and tired after exerting myself for nearly 13-14 hours of daily duty, at times. The job which I was doing-did I like or not-was really difficult question for me to answer. But then again, that was the only job for me to do or was that I felt so? I was spending almost 4 to 5 hours commuting between work and home when I had to go to Toronto. That was my second job. Both the jobs were temporary, part time jobs for few months. I wasn't sure when they will end and what would be next?

Although, I was working for long hours and trying to do the best from my side, the people whom I had to deal with at workplaces weren't supportive. A harmonious work environment was totally missing at my workplace. In a way, it was a typical non-conducive, toxic environment full of unhappy and unsatisfied people. I was duty-bound to do rewardless, boring jobs which were killing my creativity, positivity and knowledge, per se. There was no significant monetary gain too. There was no job satisfaction at all. Although my students were appreciating my efforts and assistance, not a single day I could be truly happy and looking forward going to work. There was a constant nagging feeling that I was torturing myself, and for what?!

The journey of my life from 2011 to 2015 was literally a rollercoaster ride for me and admittedly, with more lows than highs. I constantly felt I'd been to hell and back. There were more days and months of sinking spirit than mounted spirit. "Would I ever be able to change the trajectory of my life the way it's going through at this juncture of my life?" was the question persistently bugging my head. Honestly, I didn't think I would. I was utterly skeptic with no confidence left in me.

Time and time again, I was missing my blissful past when I used to work in medical universities. The life was very happy, content and full of job-satisfaction. "Where is that vivacious psychiatry professor?" my aching heart constantly asked me. I was getting a feeling of being lost in an alien world with no clue for what to do to keep myself creative, useful and contented. My past was greatly fulfilling for me and imitable for others, per se. My glorious past was what I was missing at this juncture.

"NEVER FALL BEFORE THE FALL AND ALWAYS RISE AFTER THE FALL". I was constantly encouraging myself against all odds that I was passing through.

CHAPTER 8

PAST

While looking back to the bygone era, I recollected my prestigious and fulfilling work experiences in various academic, administrative and clinical fields of medicine. That was the period before the year 2011.

All through the years of my professional life, I've had tried to be a good human being and help others in my best of the capabilities. The professional commitment was a great challenge, yet very fulfilling. Amidst all professional responsibilities and personal commitments, life was pretty much peaceful and running at a great consistent pace. There were many ups and downs, but not so devastating. I've had great experience of working in various medical universities and colleges across the globe, attended a great number of conferences, professional meetings and shared my expertise in diverse fields of modern medicine and business administrations. I'd a great say in many of professional advisory boards and communities as well.

Apart from psychiatry, I'd a great medical and clinical research practice spanning more than 30 years in my lap. I'd successfully run 50-100 operatory settings in big hospitals and have had trained more than few thousands of students in various global universities. After starting the professional career in medicine field at the age of 23, my career and I had come a long way. I'd achieved meritorious position in the university in final year of my medicine graduation, and subsequently first division in my post grad-specialty, which had paved a way for me to a dream career of my choice.

My academic excellence has had fetched me great career positions and opportunities any scholar would dream of. I was always satisfied with my achievements and success. I remained excited for new developments and ventures in my professional fields at all levels.

I'd worked as a Head of the department and professor in various prestigious medical institutions world over from 1998 to 2010. I was invited as a key-note speaker in many international conferences, seminars and chaired session on global professional arena. I'd organized various conferences in the capacity of an organizing secretary, head of institution and chairperson during the years of 2001 to 2010. The same period brought me great opportunity to serve in the capacity of Post Grad guide for specialty programs in the field of medicine for postdoctoral students in various well-known universities.

I had a great number of publications and presentations on my name. I also wrote and published few textbooks and number of write ups in the field of medicine. I became a successful author and writer through my successful publications. I was proud of myself owing to my zeal of achieving professional excellence, perseverance and hard-working attitude. All through my professional career, I was genuinely loved and respected by my fraternity colleagues, pear group, students and others.

In the year 2006, I received a prestigious fellowship from the highest professional body in USA for my meritorious achievement, contribution to the profession and community service activities. The subsequent years I won a couple of awards for the professional activities and contributions in the field. I became the chief editor for some prestigious medical journals. In the year 2009, I was invited to be on the editorial boards of certain South Asian federation professional publications. I visited countries like Japan, South Korea, Malaysia, and Singapore to discuss new-fangled developments in professional fields. From 2005 to 2011, I attained high level position with great wages in few countries in Northern African continent and Middle east. Same years, I also organized and conducted scientific sessions in Asian and some European countries.

I'd worked very hard for what I'd achieved, and I was proud of. My Image, my personality or my achievements, although I'd acquired through my own efforts and hard work, were enough to trigger professional envy in others. All through those years I lived a near picture perfect life. I'd succeeded in getting whatever I've had ever dreamt of, despite fighting all odds. By the time I turned 45, I was moving at high speed consistently and persistently increasing the radius of my achievements with a great stable center.

If I look back now and try to think about my life trajectory, it seems to me as if looking at a mesmerizing mountain range or magnificent rows of exotic flowers in a garden!

By the end of 2010, I already had worked at major important professional positions and had attained phenomenal professional success. Obviously, I was very happy and content with my life. Although there were many ups and downs in my personal and professional life, I remained winner in most conditions. I never got overwhelmed by my success and never lost my patience in failures. I trusted divinity and inner strength in all situations. Life was a wonderful bliss, beyond my own dreams and fancies. Eternal bliss with vibrant color was reflecting in my persona, appearance and existence. Certainly, I couldn't have asked for more.

Toward the end of the year 2011, I moved to Ontario, Canada, the number one country to live and raise the family. Canada has been always ranked as the most beautiful country in the world, and also it has been hailed for its quality of life as per the various world reports published time and time again.

CHAPTER 9

NEW BEGINNING- LATER 2011

In the early 2011, I received a registered letter from the Canadian immigration authorities congratulating me and my family for availing the dream opportunity to immigrate to Canada. Probably, it was the month of April. It was the much-awaited response to our family file application which I'd applied somewhere in the year 2004. It took long time to take final decision. It had been processed now and as per the great news we were all now set to move to one of the most wonderful countries on this earth! Luck has prevailed, I felt very happy and so was my family. The way had been paved for us to finally immigrate to Canada.

Everyone, especially my 3 kids- 2 sons and a daughter were very elated upon receiving the news and enthusiastically started preparation for a new life in the new country. My husband was excited too. My parents were happy for me and my family.

"Life would be definitely better in Canada compared to India for all of you, especially your kids, you must go!" My parents opined.

All were happy. What was my take?

Of course, it was a major, critical decision to make for me, per se. My husband and I were working in a high position in one of the best, reputed Medical Universities of Asia that time. We both were enjoying our professional and personal lives. We both had authoritative and influential positions with great work, great perks and great job satisfaction. It was not that simple and easy to give up those rewards associated with our professional positions.

However, Canada has had great, world-wide reputation, we felt the same time. Temptation to stay was at par with the temptation to leave for better opportunities. Whether to continue at or to leave our present positions- was difficult to decide. It was a tough decision for both of us. Nonetheless, our kids were our priority and raising the kids in Canada would fetch better development and opportunities for them, we felt. Hence, we decided to immigrate as soon as possible. Immigration process had its own hurdles and quandaries. After passing through somewhat demanding, complex immigration processes, we became successful in getting our PR status in Canada.

Within next 6-8 months' period, we were in Canada- The dream land of many in the world!

Although we had landed successfully in Canada, we were a bit anxious and unsure about our future moves and professional career. I did some homework in relation with our settlement processes in new land. We were not much clear about how and where to start our new life, though.

Our kids were very much excited to be Canadians and so were I and my husband. My extended family was too curious to learn about our progress in Canada. In back home, they all were eagerly waiting for our successful establishment in Canada.

That was the time we all were unified in our thought processes, our desires, our dreams, our actions, and our decisions. But I was oblivious to the fact that that was the last phase of my life when all of us were cohesive and standing together!

The year of 2011 became the period in my life which changed

everything in my life—my whole life, including everything within me! My life trajectory took an unprecedented, unanticipated, turn thereupon.

That sudden change in my life trajectory led to mega changes in my living perspectives as well as huge differences in the outcomes I got in my next half of life.

CHAPTER 10

Life was a constant struggle since I moved in here in 2011. It'd been over 3 years now living and feeling as a very part of Canada, still a lot more was missing in my life. The life was not same as it was before. It was totally a different life with diverse issues-good and bad.

My husband and I tried to put our best foot forward to establish our personal and professional lives overcoming all teething troubles and glitches of mundane life in a new place. We'd embarked on an undertaking with as many efforts and determination as possible. We both were working hard. Our determination and resolution were strong to make mark in this world as well after attaining accomplished professional careers with high social status in other parts of the world. Living life as a Canadian wasn't easy for us, though. Against all odds and hardships of life, I was trying to remain optimistic and believed in revolutionary approach since as a futuristic thinker, I believed in the ability to look past the events of today and into the possibilities of tomorrow.

Juggling between 2 to 3 part-time jobs in a day and then home, I was hardly getting any time for myself. The kids were grown up individuals now. They were in universities and busy in their own worlds. Their demands and requirements were increasing day by day. Life was more demanding and challenging for them too, all of us had realized by then. Their desires and dreams were different from those of their parents. Expectations were higher than what can be fulfilled reasonably. Expenses were very high and income sources were very limited. We were literally using our savings to survive in dignified ways.

Unprecedented migration of people around the globe in search of work in the modern times has ever had a widespread and troubling result: the separation of families. Ours was the classic example of this phenomenon!

The consequence of all our problems and sufferings was obvious and reflecting clearly in our lives. The family bond had gotten loose. The distance between the hearts was also growing gradually. The cohesiveness in the family was missing. Obviously, every one of us was living in their own small world, by choice or by fate. I was feeling torn apart between myself and fulfillment of my family needs.

Working hard was a requirement to achieve the professional and financial levels I was at before. I wanted to prove myself. I wasn't required to prove anyone else but, it was a promise to self. After achieving certain level in life, you don't require to testify or to show your capabilities to people, that was my take. Nonetheless, you don't want to succumb to the pressure of adversities in life and loose self-esteem and confidence in your own eyes. Falling from the grace could never be accepted by any means- I strongly believed.

Hard work has never been an issue for me. I'm used to multitask and hard work. Managing extremely busy work life and home life was a real issue, though. Work hours were totally inconsistent and what I was getting in the end was frustration because of temporary work opportunity and constant job insecurity. There was nothing like a permanent job, I'd realized in short time. There was no job opportunity in universities or in fields of psychiatry or clinical research. There were only part-time and temporary jobs for me, may or may not be related with my field of qualification or expertise. I wasn't interested to waste my time in survival jobs, per se. Education and healthcare were my fields of expertise and I was determined to be in my professional fields.

It was mandatory for me to keep learning new knowledge in diverse fields. I was happy to learn new things, in general. Not all times it was a pleasant experience, though. It required lots of time, efforts, energy and focus to adapt to new knowledges and skills in diverse fields alien to me such as accounting, economics, math, physics, or business strategies. It was cumbersome to study and gain expertise in such subject knowledge; however, it was needed to get decent job positions in education field. The new gained information needed constant update too. After some time, new knowledge in other fields would be required. It was an endless game. I was feeling frustrated!

At times, I was without work for continuous 4-5 months despite looking for job and ready to work at any professional level. Nonetheless, living on social welfare or employment insurance was out of purview for a person like me believing in self-reliance and having hardworking attitude. Sitting home idly was absolutely beyond consideration; unthinkable.

"Welcome to the Land of Challenges!" I could remember my friend welcoming me to Canada who immigrated here few years back. I'd realized the essence of that sentence by now!

People say you must come out of your comfort zone to achieve success in life. Here I was in the situation where I'd embarked upon a journey that was totally out of my comfort zone! I was a below average person fallen from the grace of an extraordinary status. I constantly felt trapped and stuck up in a position that didn't do any good to me. At times, I would spend nearly 5 hours a day commuting on the busiest roads and streets and some of the most dangerous highways of GTA, putting myself at risk, but for what? I had no good answer to that.

I do agree that earning money is important in life, nevertheless, the older a person gets, the more he or she starts to realize that your TIME is more precious than any money you earn, especially, if the money is not providing you with the much-needed happiness of inside as well as the job satisfaction. That was me.

I started hating my life. I was feeling dejected every morning and every evening, every day and every night. I was feeling a sort of being rejected by everyone. I was like exhausted and tired of everything in life. Getting out of bed seemed like a daunting task. Every morning, I'd wake up and think that I'd have to go through this hell one more day. Each day felt meaningless. I felt drained all the time.

I got failed 6 times in my driving tests, which was unbelievable! I had spent lots of money, time and energy in preparing myself for getting the driving license in past three years. Having a valid driver license had been a necessity by then to travel reasonably comfortable way in and out the city. I also took driving lessons to pass, but all in vain. Looking at the fact that I'd an excellent record of driving on the busiest streets and foremost roads of few countries without a single incident of accident or fender-bender, it was distressful to get repeated failures in driving tests in here. I felt extremely low. There was a sense of lot of unknown, unexplained guilt within. I never felt so helpless and miserable in my life, even while confronting most adversities on the trajectory of life.

There was a constant war in my mind- between my past and present, which disturbed me a lot. I've had worked very hard all my life. I'd held some great positions in various parts of the world, had earned some great wages, and been a part of some amazing projects. Something, nonetheless, remained always the same — looking for the job satisfaction while looking forward to going to work every day. As a hard-working professional, I was punctual, dependable, diligent in laboring, and that was appreciated by all in my workplace. More than money, I'd earned as remuneration- great respect, grace and happiness. Now, I was trading my time for the money. I was a reputed psychiatrist, who never got sick, now my stress was killing me! The tragic reality was hurting me a lot.

At this juncture of my life, I'd come to comprehend that the money come and go but time is something one can never get back. I was working day and night for what? Money- really? I wasn't sure even. The money was too small in exchange of my time, efforts and energy I was putting into the jobs I was doing. Top of all, there was no appreciation of my efforts, honesty and integrity. I was putting my heart into the accomplishment of my duties and responsibilities, none even cared. It was so hurtful. I was feeling pity for myself the way whole day and night I was working. I was really wasting my time and my life, I felt.

"We ain't happy one bit in what you're doing in present scenario, you must figure out the next step of your life." My mind and my heart were on the path of revolt with me.

Despite the persistent conflicts between my mind and my thought processes, my family wasn't aware of what was going on with me and my life. I was utterly mystified by the way my life was moving in the unknown direction at faster pace. Nevertheless, I was wearing different mask to exhibit artificial happiness and joy to my parents, relatives and friends.

CHAPTER 11

DISCOVERING SOCIAL ANXIETY- SEPTEMBER 2015

I could vaguely remember that was a 2nd Thursday in the September month. It was an Anatomy and Physiology class for the 2nd year premedical students at Caribbean Medical University. It was the fall semester, 2015. I was teaching that batch of the students for two semesters. That was my another part-time job.

There were 10 students in that group. They were intelligent and hardworking students, who loved me and enjoyed my teaching. I got along with them very well. We shared lots of knowledge and information with fun activities in the class. It was a first class after the summer break of 2 months. The students were happy and excited to be back to school. It wasn't all well my side, though. I was feeling awful with no apparent reason. Depression was making me think too much introspectively, what I was trying to avoid that time.

I was discussing about the nervous system and fight-or-flight response as a physiological reaction occurring in response to a perceived harmful event or threat to survival. In the middle of the discussion, I started feeling strange with my body. I started trembling.

"Oh no, I'm shaking!" I realized. "What's that?" No idea.

I took deep breath. More shaking, tense muscles, feeling of palpitations. I started panicking!

I was standing and conducting the lecture. I immediately drew chair lying nearby close to me. I sat down in the chair and remained still for a while. I was experiencing twitching, trembling and shaky feelings. I firmly tried to control my shaking, hiding my hands behind my back, hiding from others. Unfortunately, fighting against my anxiety and using avoidance strategies tended to make my shaking worse. I was going through terrible feelings. I felt fearful for no reason. I felt hopeless, nothing seemed to make sense at that moment.

All the bad things of my past started roaming in my mind, scaring me for the worst future for me. I felt dreadful! I got a dry mouth. No matter what I did, I couldn't get my mind off my problems.

Was my life such bad? To prevent embarrassment and hide feelings, I immediately rushed to the washroom. I spent some time wondering why I was feeling the way I did.

'What should I do- continue the class or leave for the day?' I was clueless.

I was struggling with social anxiety disorder—I soon realized; one more addition to my existing stress, anxiety and depression list!

I was shaking in front of others. I found I'd trouble raising a glass to my lips or holding notes during a lecture without shaking. I even noticed my legs were constantly shaking and also my lips were quivering. My muscles were tense, aching, and sore.

'These days, I am a changed one. When someone snaps at me, I spend the rest of the day thinking about it. For last few days, I was avoiding dealing with a group of people.' I started thinking about my changed behavior and lifestyle. Often, I avoided my social media interactions due to unknown fears. I was a social person, per se and enjoyed interacting with people in general. However, I was avoiding use of Facebook, WhatsApp and other social media now. The telephone ringing would scare me to death due to strange fears! The person on the other end would threaten me or kill me, was the fear looming large all the time. I was getting frequent nightmares. I constantly felt tense or on edge. Often my symptoms were going by a cycle of negative thinking. I was thinking too much and also too much negative.

'Everyone gets nervous from time to time', I tried to pacify myself that very juncture. My shaking should not have any negative effect on my daily functioning, I wanted to make sure. Also, No one should know about my mental health issue, I was more concerned about that time.

I spent nearly half an hour inside the washroom. I cried loudly for few minutes which made me feel a bit lighter. I splashed my face repeatedly with cold water to refresh myself before going back to the class. I was feeling better. My students and their jovial company helped a great deal in getting me back to my normal self.

I felt terrible that evening on the way back home. I was struggling with social anxiety disorder apart from depression and anxiety and losing self-control!

Whole night, I kept sobbing and crying in my bed, feeling pitiably small, totally in low spirits from loss of any hope or courage. I was continuously resisting urge to harm myself or commit suicide or something-anything which could set me free from my miseries or take me away from my plight that point of time. While in bed, crying every 20 minutes, I would look up at wall clock and start crying again because the night was not going to end soon.

One more terribly long night had ended at an agonizingly slow pace.

CHAPTER 12

TURBULENT LIFE-
OCTOBER 2015

The days and nights were passing amidst trepidation and uncertainty. Night sweats became a regular feature. Nightmares also became a regular occurrence. I was aware that anxiety, stress and emotional problems that cause sweating during the day can often have the same effect at night. But that was not just the case.

Due to over exertion linked to work related activities; I developed severe pain in my lower back and left leg. The pain was radiating in nature, referring to entire left lower extremity, frequently getting moderate to severe in kind. Top of all, constant lack of sleep, nightmares and negative thoughts during the day, lack of job satisfaction, constant feeling of unhappiness had affected my physical and mental health vary badly.

I visited my family doctor for my physical assessment and pain. She referred me for ultrasound, x-rays and CT Scans. I got my reports in 2 weeks. My scans and X-rays were showing severe defect in my L5-S1 vertebra. The condition was diagnosed as Anterolisthesis or spondylosis. Aging is generally considered to be a common cause of anterolisthesis, which occurs naturally over time as the cartilage between vertebrae weakens and thins. Nevertheless, constant pressure on my legs due to long standing hours and inadequate rest during work activities had impacted my condition significantly, the doctor explained me in detail.

I was required to take good care of my spinal cord and back in order to prevent further damage to my shoulders and lower back. I was advised to control my weight (thanks to my changed erratic diet-timings and junk food habits) as reduction of weight on the lower extremities could help decrease pain intensity. But where was the much-needed rest? I was responsible for putting myself in that situation, I felt.

I'd problem with my eyes too. I was feeling blurred vision and fatigue in my eyes for last 6 months, for reason unknown to me. My ophthalmologist advised me not to overstrain my eyes to prevent any internal problem which may require surgical intervention.

A couple of months back, I got severe dental ache in my upper jaw. My dentist took my full mouth x-ray and diagnosed with suspected periapical pathosis in an upper tooth requiring a root canal therapy. Three of my lower teeth started aching soon after, I am not quite sure, whether that was—a butterfly effect or a domino effect, where a cumulative effect was produced with one event initiated a succession of similar events like ripple effects. All problems one after another were increasing day by day in magnitude and propensity, I noted.

My different body pains were scaring the hell out of me, for sure. Every body part was conspiring against me, I felt.

Event after event had gone traumatic in last few years. Time was flying at high speed amidst all sad memories.

I had lost many people and things in my life. Last year, I lost my dear father. I couldn't physically meet him in last 6 years due to living in another country as well as my overly busy schedule and mundane responsibilities. Last few months, due to his sickness, he was unable to talk with me on phone, which he used to do regularly before his sickness. He was the best friend of mine, with whom I could talk and discuss anything on this planet. He would guide me, direct me, and advise me on every front. I was missing him very badly. The pain of losing him was tremendous and troubling my soul every day!

I've had best nostalgic memories of my childhood. We had a very well-knit family of 12 members at my parent's house. From my parent's big family to my own small family, I'd come a long way. Mostly, I was staying alone these days, though.

My daughter had moved out with her boyfriend nearly 3 years back. My elder son got married soon after and lived far away with his family. It had been couple of years now I was living like this. Rocky, my dog was the best member of my family, I was proud of. After my father's demise, memories from my childhood were returning in a pronounced manner.

While thinking about the life losses, the pain and agonies were tremendous of the loss, demise and separation in life. I was missing my sweet home, my family, my birth country, my clinical practice, my established career, my friends... the list was long. At that very juncture, whom and what was I missing was not clear in my mind, though.

Due to all those emotions and sentiments, waking up in the middle of the night and crying like a baby was quite disturbing. I found it very difficult to comfort the child within. I wanted someone to actually give her a hug (mentally, but with true feelings).

Someone could say, "I love you. It isn't your fault, and you don't deserve all these pains. Don't worry. All will be alright".

I was very much concerned for the whole mess created in the past few years of my life. At one point of time, I blamed others for my suffering. Other time, I felt myself accountable. I was responsible for all of my actions, happenings and my life as a whole, when I got that realization; I decided to clear the mess by all means. But how? And when?

My negativity and sinking spirit were behind my plight and I was feeling vulnerable. I'd lost my focus, my vision, my creativity and positivity amidst confusion. My fears, my trepidation, my depressive state, my anxiety and uncertainty about future were gripping my mind and my discipline. I was convinced about loss of self-control and will power in whole chaos. I found myself inept doing any small thing that may require deliberate cognition.

I was looking for patterns- anything to make me feel less trapped, like I had control. I couldn't enjoy concerts or festivals or bars because there are too many people–what if there's a fire? What if someone starts shooting? Will I get crushed to death in the inevitable stampede? Lots of constant fears were plaguing my mind.

I was changed. I was refraining from commenting or talking about mentally challenged people. I stopped watching movies on mental health, which was a favorite topic of mine few years back. I also avoided watching any program related with psychiatry or psychologically affected people.

The term 'mental' was driving me crazy, the sad fact I realized when one day someone was talking about a mentally challenged patient. I strongly felt that I would end up in that situation if I would continue listening about or seeing such people! It was really very scary feeling. I was also avoiding talking about old people—what if I become old suddenly by talking about them? Or what will happen to me when I will grow old? I'd developed gerontophobia (fear of old) and gerascophobia (anxieties/fear of growing old). The fear of getting old, ugly and unwanted was providing me horrendous feelings inside me, which were getting stronger day by day.

Nostalgia became a source of suffering for me at one point of time. It was causing me symptoms such as palpitations, anxiety, insomnia, and disturbed eating habits. My nostalgic feelings were like a mental disorder like my depression. I avoided listening to nostalgic melodious music, which always stirred my heart and beautiful romantic feelings in me. Instead, now I preferred to listen new generation, new hip-hop songs, which I never had any appetite for, per se. This was a drastic change in me. That sudden change of liking and disliking things was actually attributed to and reflecting my deep-seated anxiety and cry for help, I realized it when I came out of that terrible phase of my life.

Although I've never been a strong religious being, I'm an individual with prolific spiritual inclination and belief. Hence, I always felt guilty for not being divinely healed of my depression and anxiety. I could vividly remember the phase of suffering of my life when I used to pray Almighty to heal me and free me from the cruel clutches of those devastating demons of depression and anxiety. On the contrary, I used to get horrendous feelings of powerlessness since I could see those demons fighting strenuously with my God too, defeating God's power of healing. It was unbelievable and appalling! That was shocking and distressful for me.

It was out of my wildest dream that my faith could fail to protect me from negativity and evil spirits! The power of depression and anxiety had completely demonized my mind, I was experiencing the strong effects.

My family and friends understand me, but to a point. They could sympathize but may not empathize. Mental illness is still a stigma in traditional cultures, where I belong. Discussions of mental health problems or mental illness is taboo, due to a cultural perspective that mental illnesses signify being 'crazy' or 'mad,' thereby preventing families from seeking help because of fear of bringing shame on the family.

I deliberately refrained from discussing my mental health issues with any of my friends or acquaintances, assuming that may not understand what I was going through. Moreover, it would be beyond their imagination that a strong-willed person such as me, a doctor could suffer from 'mental' problem! I remembered one of my childhood friends suffered from depression and how the people reacted to her condition. Most people were unsupportive. They were like "everyone's going through one thing or another, so take it easy. "You ain't a special one. Stop wearing your feelings on your sleeve; other people have got worse issues." That had made her very sad and dejected. It was me this time.

At times, I had strong feeling that death was the only way out for me and commit suicide and be done with life but couldn't voice it out. I'd prefer to sleep forever to get rid of my situation but thought about my grief-stricken family and friends after me.

I tried to avoid undue visit to my regular doctor as well and tried to hide my real feelings by saying 'I'm fine' to avoid unnecessary discussion and feelings of being down with something terrible in life. I'd developed the feeling of dejection that —nobody really cared for me. Everyone was busier and happier than me and problem free. There were no more "happy days" for me, even if few moments I got, they'd not last long, for sure.

I hated to work but I needed to. I could not see the future! The worst thing was-people asking me about my health. The typical simple question" how are you doing" used to piss me off, literally! Such small, unintentional formality used to unnerve me a lot. I felt awkward to answer it with nothing other than negativity on my side, per se. I was factually avoiding public interaction. Anxiety had dug a big negative groove in my brain and had made it impossible to hang on to a positive thought for more than 5 seconds. Most devastating effect was on my self-esteem as that the ability to see the multifaceted personality of my own self was lost. My vision became very narrow. Everything I did or tried to do was leading me to pessimism or negative outcome. I got locked into a narrow view of who I was and had lost the sight of my own possibilities.

Quite few nights I spent sleeping on my floor directly avoiding sleeping underneath the ceiling fan. I couldn't sleep for hours because I imagined what I would do if the ceiling fan suddenly collapsed. I also preferred to keep my bedroom door open at night due to strange fears—what if at night something happened to me? What if in night someone attacked me and killed me? What if an earthquake occurred at night? The other night, I made some plans to protect myself in different situations, if something goes wrong, and went over the plans again and again, all night long!

CHAPTER 13

DEALING WITH DEPRESSION
AND ANXIETY-NOVEMBER 2015

According to the Anxiety and Depression Association of America, anxiety disorders are the most prevalent mental health condition in Northern America, and over 40 million adults are afflicted with the condition. Anxiety disorders are among the most common types of mental disorders world over and have been shown to have a major impact on the daily lives of the sufferers.

In 2013, an estimated 3 million Canadians (11.6%) aged 18 years or older reported having a mood and/or anxiety disorder. Same year, I used to share detailed knowledge of depression, anxiety disorder and their effects on lives of individuals suffering from them with my students.

"When one is really anxious, their thinking center may shrink to a minuscule size. It's understandably hard to feel good about self when anxiety disrupts our focus and concentration, leaving us incompetent to perform even normal daily activities. It makes us incapable to take in new information, read, write, study, analyze, or concentrate. Anxiety sucks, being isolated and believing that your family or friends don't care for you sucks even more. Even when they do, you remain steadfast to believe no one cares for you." I explained them.

In most scenarios, I avoided going out with anyone. I was very much like confided to self. At times, I'd a small outing planned, or a coffee meeting with my friends or colleagues at work and suddenly the four walls of my house seemed to me the only safe haven because it'd be the only secured place, I'd not have to pretend that everything is fine with me. Consequently, I'd simply cancel going out with them. At times, I preferred to make an excuse of having already busy that weekend or that holiday when I was invited out. I'd pretend to be terribly sorry for not being able to accompany them and enjoy their company. Ironically, that time I was actually just busy holding it together in my comfort zone or crying for long hours in isolation!

Stray thoughts of gerontophobia, loss of self-control, feelings of uselessness and insignificant to others too used to scare me severely and constantly. Often, while walking down the streets or driving on the roads if I saw any car pulled over by the police, it freaked me out for no reason. I feared as if cops would handcuff me and would arrest me may be for improper walking or driving! It was really crazy and scary!

Anxiety was like a demon kept chasing me due to my weaker mind and loss of confidence, my guess. When I was a teenage, I'd a friend exhibiting anxiety. Self-sabotage was a side effect of her anxiety problem in different situations of life. I could even recall while going to a party or a gathering, she felt extremely anxious and found it difficult to talk to other kids. She worried ceaselessly that she would end up in hell if she made a single mistake. She could get anxiety about nearly anything and everything—until she turned 20. People teased her by calling 'crazy coocoo'. She was good in her studies but, often got trouble focusing on studies. We lost contact after schooling. Despite her mental health issue, she could pursue in engineering profession and also made a name for herself in writing career. I was always curious how she could manage to do all notwithstanding her psychological condition.

I never had any mental health issue during my younger days. I maintained my perfect image intact for years. It was a reality, not a fake portrayal- unlike this time. I was trying to maintain my perfect image; but depression was moving a step ahead of me. I was trying to behave normal yet there was my anxiety, undermining my important moments. I tried to ignore it many times.

Self-destruction was a chief side effect of my failing mental health reflecting in different situations in my life now. At that juncture, I recollected the tragic suicide incident of one of my university students suffering from chronic depression and anxiety. No one believed him when he confined to his best friends about his sufferings. Considering his great intelligence and bright medical career, need for psychological therapy seemed to be out of question for others. He really wanted help for his problems, nonetheless, others misunderstood him and failed to provide him with support, love and care that time. He was unable to express the voice inside his head and eventually chose the path to end his life!

After considerable difficulties in the various stages of my conditions, my anxiety and accompanying depression were worse than ever. I knew I needed help but asking for help was against my basic nature. It just made me feel like crippled. I didn't want to indulge in meds and doctors routine. I felt as if I had lost myself and wouldn't ever be the same again. I was left with no motivation at all to do anything because I couldn't see a future for myself.

Anxiety caused me to believe everyone was faking their love for me. 'Cheer up' was the worst thing anyone could have said to me that point of time. Those two words triggered thousands of horrible thoughts. I was pretty much baffled and directionless. I wanted to be happy, cheerful and joyous- an original myself- but I couldn't. I wanted to be free of my negative thoughts. I wanted everyone to know how I felt but I didn't dare tell them. Eventually, I just isolated myself in my room because no contact with people meant nothing could go wrong. I felt so.

'You must face your deepest fears, or you'll always be a slave to them', I read somewhere. I wanted to follow it. My path wasn't unusual: People with anxiety disorders often resist therapy, feeling they should be able to manage on their own. Talk therapy is believed to be effective in treating all types of anxiety. When I was at my lowest point, my inner self got agitated to find out the solution to my problems. My thoughts were contradictory-some convinced me to make myself strong and fight full throttle with willpower and determination, others were forcing me to do the one thing that would end up changing everything—the thing I had been resisting for no good reason; to go for psychotherapy!

I was still not ready to believe and accept that I needed therapy-psychotherapy or counselling. I had strong desire and resolve to succeed in that agonizing battle with my demons, though. I decided to talk to someone, who can not only provide me professional guidance but also care for me, understand me and guide me as a special friend. Until now, none in my family or friends was aware of what I was going through. None would even believe me, since I wasn't the same what they were familiar with! All knew me as a dedicated and oriented but, happy-go-lucky individual, who always enjoyed whatever she did and enjoyed the life every bit. I wasn't that person anymore, for sure.

Next day after completion of my class, I called my psychiatrist friend in US, whom I felt to be the best person to look for help. It'd been a while since we spoke. When I called her, she seemed to be excited to talk about her success stories and also listen to my achievements since our last contact. I became a bit open with her, with some hesitation. I tried to explain my situation and asked for her friendly advice.

Initially, she laughed at my narrative and refused to believe that I was the real patient! She opined that being a psychiatrist and positive minded person like me could never get mental problems. Her conviction and belief about my professional competency and strong-willed character made me more conscious about self-esteem. I didn't want to lose my value in her eyes. I'd genuine apprehension regarding full recovery from my mental health issue and chances of relapse. Hence, I made up a story of someone suffering from depression and anxiety, needing just another professional opinion to help her out.

I wanted her sympathetic response boosting my moral at that juncture, indirectly. After listening me, she advised my (imaginary) patient to go right away for a psychiatric counselling and full course medication, emphasizing side effects of the medications. She also stressed that relapse chances could be high in situation like that of my patient!

Her strong forewarning tone of voice scared the hell out of me! That wasn't the solution, I wanted. What I wanted-indirectly-from her was- 'Yes, you can, and you will'- a strong motivational approach to conquer and get full recovery from the dreaded situation. I desired she could say, "Don't worry; everything will be fine. Nothing bad happens in such cases and full recovery is always possible. There is no chance of relapse."

I felt totally disappointed and lost. Our talk got concluded on a sad note. I didn't let her know that, though.

I wanted at that juncture, someone who could bring the 'real-positive' me out of that 'demon infested-negative' me. I again felt miserable that night and tried to revert to myself for help. I strongly felt no one else, but I have to help myself. I must find out the way. Sooner will be better.

CHAPTER 14

When things go out of proportion, new developments may take place. By the February of 2016, the things had truly gone wild my side. Life had been a total mess and curse for me. All through this, I'd turned very sad, pessimistic and dejected. My mind was totally possessed by a giant devil called depression, accompanied by another devil- Anxiety disorder. Both had sneaked into my otherwise peaceful life, managed to get strong hold of it, sabotaged my inner and outer peace and had completely ruined my happy existence. I was living on the edge. At times, I was like close to being frightened or overreacting to a small thing and losing temper. My behavior was difficult to be comprehended even by me.

According to studies the number of people suffering from at least one anxiety disorder during the course of their lives is staggering. I was feeling I was going through multiple. I had symptoms of a couple of companion disorders, too. I had self-diagnosed obsessive-compulsive disorder, hypochondria, PTSD and what not. I would feel a sense of creepy fear now and then. I agonized over every strange sensation or pang of physical pain. A mild headache was plainly a cerebral stroke, a small mole was melanoma, and a bruise was cancer!

The nights were horrible and sweaty out of fears. Every so often some kind of phobia would erupt at the base of my spine and travel upward. My heart rate would shoot up at night and I felt the erratic sounds pounding against my ears and my eyes would go blind. My breathing would turn erratically shallow and fast. My stomach would rumble at unforeseen things, and I break out in a pool of sweat.

At times, I felt I probably was behaving like an old curmudgeon- more grumpy, cantankerous and gloomy. My present job and type of work were major contributors to my prevailing situation- a bone of contention, so to speak. It was a total misfit and I simply hated the job I was doing, which was a strenuous work literally sucking everything out of my body and spirit, I felt. It was a terribly monotonous routine with no chance of any pleasurable change, positive professional or personal development, encouragement or promotion. It was a stagnated, stinking life.

Our freedom is more important than any amount of money or material possession, I believed. But I'd turned into a machine with no vitality. My verve and vigor were lost. It was a terrible mix of claustrophobic and cleithrophobic feelings. I was feelings like crying, screaming, physically lashing out, freezing up, and attempting to run away. There was the feeling of being locked in a windowless room with no escape at one end and the fear of being trapped and constant fear of panic attacks the other end.

There was simply nothing to look forward to any given day for me, that was what most troubled me. Days were passing amidst- artificially mounted spirit one day and naturally sinking spirit the other day!

I could still remember those days, while flipping through the pages of the calendar in my office room, I used to do self-talk. I felt like the time was flying at a much rapid pace. "I don't want to work like this. I don't want to continue further in this job. This job is a killer for me. I'm sure going to die some day in a small dingy corner of this office like no one ever knew me." My overly tired body and aching heart were constantly complaining.

Time flies, whether you're wasting it or not. Yes, for me, time was flying very fast, with literally no productivity and no personal gain and satisfaction of life.

At that very juncture, I wasn't sure what I wanted to do in my life, actually. I wasn't sure what would be my next step if I leave that job and work? Who will help me in my decision to do something other than that job? What could be the plan A and Plan B? And top of all, what would those plans be? Nothing was sure. My vision was very dim. In fact, there was no vision, per se. Nevertheless, what I knew that point in time was-what I didn't want to do. I just wanted to come out of that quagmire, get out of that killer work routine. Yes, I was determined to do anything in life other than pursuing in the same killer job who had literally killed my self-esteem and vitality.

The days were passing- one after another, I was getting older day by day, with my dreams dying inside my imaginations and brain. My job, my work, probably I too—all were killing them. My happiness and satisfaction in life were of paramount importance for me which I was unable to provide to myself. The frustration and dejection were soaring.

Where There's A Will, There's A Way- March 2016

Finally, I got that "Put your foot down" moment that changed my life. That was the moment-when after many-many days, nights, months of trepidation, torture, and torments, I was determined to help myself, to reinvent myself, and to bring back my original self.

'Enough is enough'- finally one fine day my agitated heart revolted against my status quo which I'd maintained all through those past few years. I put my foot down when I had lost all my patience waiting for some 'magic to happen'. 'I would not carry on like this.' I decided. I was all set to refuse to endorse negativity prevailing in my life and was getting ready to invite back vibrancy and vitality in my gloomy life. I strongly wanted to streamline areas of my life that were repetitive and annoying. I was determined to carve out time for the things that were more important in my life. I wanted to optimize my life. Having said that, I knew it was not all that easy. It was also about revitalizing how I was spending my time-at home and at work. I wanted to make sure that I treat every single minute of my life as a precious moment that I could pay all my attention. I knew I needed to get organized but didn't know where to start. Decluttering, simplify, and streamline my life were on my priority list.

"I wanted to be happy and want to see you too happy and confident now" when my aggrieved heart reprimanded me, to be honest, I liked it. I instantaneously appreciated the deep concern expressed by my heart, my inner consciousness.

My realization time had arrived. I desperately wanted to see myself turning into a 'eagerly looking forward to' person from a hopeless, miserable, pessimistic person. I knew that moment would be the great moment-a turning point in life-for me! I was desperately waiting for the one.

Amidst all my miseries and negative thought processes of my ailing mind, I had a faint voice of confidence inside me which was constantly saying, you can do it. "You are bold enough to tackle this issue on your own. You have to help yourself. You can do that. Find out the way to come out victoriously from this quagmire. And trust this, it will never happen again to you. Be courageous and fight it back." Saintly side of mine was determined to win over my dreadful demons. "You will win, you must win!"

It was very traumatic reality for me that the teaching, preaching and unsolicited advices on positive thinking which once I used to do for others, today I'd needed them most! How strange!

But so what? Everything happens for a good reason, my positivity seemed like beaming up. My eyes shined with bright light. I was smiling with my eyes which was helping me to channel good thoughts. That moment was terrific- the beginning of a new dawn, a new era for me, I felt strong vibes of positivity and determination- a resolve to conquer my mental health issues.

I started self-talk. "You shouldn't feel guilty for feeling the way you do because depression is an illness like any other, it is similar like having a broken arm or a leg." My inner voice was constantly encouraging me. I was always told to show myself the same respect and concern that I would show for others. We are so accepting of other parts of our bodies breaking, why can't we be that way about our minds too? My psyche pleaded. It's life. I will find out the way out. I kept reassuring myself and confronting my fears and anxiety.

"Through gradual exposure to the feared situation, you'll gain a greater sense of control, and your anxiety will diminish." I told myself. My ultimate goal was to regain my self-control and be my original self- vivacious, enthusiastic, vibrant and forthcoming usual self.

I realized my problem. I needed to find out the solution now. It was challenging and testing task, for sure. I felt like living on the edge; where one side was joy and another was sorrow; where one side was bliss, and another was curse. It was like one moment; I was feeling a bit better and then very next moment it was totally miserable and dejected feeling. Nevertheless, I was determined to achieve the win. For the solution, first step was to admit the existence of problem. There was a series of actions in that protracted process.

The process involved with the solution of my problem was-understanding of Kübler-Ross model popularly known as 5 stages of grief. The 5 stages were same here- denial, anger, bargaining, depression and acceptance. Even though the model was originally designed to postulate a progression of emotional states felt by terminally ill patients, it's been represented in modern culture as model of depression. I'd been through all of them, I realized. Subsequently, I started combating strategies to restore my grace and dignity in my own eyes. The process was much slower than I imagined, and much easier said than done, though.

First step toward the solution was acceptance that I'd problem. I did. I'm really happy today that I did that at right time.

All through these years of mental agonies of depression and anxiety, I remained in denial mood to accept the reality. I could never admit that I was 'mentally' sick before. I kept suffering silently within but refused to admit that I could have life issues, especially "mental health" issues. I accepted, finally. I admitted that I'd a problem, a serious one-worst thing; but it was curable, and I would do that- the best thing!

Second step - to work upon the ways to solve it.

The main thing about my recovery process was that the only person, who could truly help me, was me. I realized the fact. I learnt to change my thought processes and stopped bullying myself. It'd be difficult initially to change my negative thought processes to positive ones, I knew, but wouldn't be impossible, I convinced myself. I started making positive changes in my lifestyle. I started reading positive thinking books and surfing various online sites guiding how to be positive and tackle our negativities. I started visiting Uplifting Sites focused on positive stories and ideas for Good living, how to be calm, how to get back lost self-control and what not. I started reading motivating stories and real-life experiences of people recovered from the psychiatric problems and those came out of depression.

I started Yoga sessions and meditation practices on my own. While confining to a room, I tried to perform all those activities and acts which can consolidate me and boost my inner strength. I wanted to kill, destroy my inner demons from the roots, who were still haunting me despite my resolve to overcome my fear, anxiety, depression and negativity. My demons were laughing upon me and confident of my defeat in the game of wining back. The process of getting back to my original, happy, and confident self was slow-a sad part, but my resolve was strong-the best part, of my story.

Self-Motivation- I made it a constant process. I started encouraging, leading and teaching myself, the way I used to teach and preach my students. I preferred the same path: counselling, understanding, motivating, inspiring myself.

Loneliness and isolation can trigger or worsen anxiety, while talking about your worries face to face can often make them seem less overwhelming. I strongly felt so. I must confine to someone. Until now I was fighting my own battle. Now I must take someone's help. Someone upon whom I can trust and rely upon for the best advice.

I asked myself-who could be that person who could help me in my problem? Someone close to me, who can guide me. Who? - My husband! My mind reminded me. My heart went with the notion instantaneously.

My husband was in Dubai on his professional assignment. He was working in the capacity of a director in a multinational company since past 3 years. It was a dream job for him. Serving at a high position, his job was very responsible and demanding in nature, though. He was supposed to be in Dubai for one more year. It'd been a couple years since we were living far away from each other. We used to see each other on occasions. We were fine with that non-permanent arrangement. It was helping us in our professional and financial growth. Finally, we had plans to be together and live comfortable life upon completion of his last international professional assignment. Until then we both were keeping ourselves occupied with work related activities. Due to our busy routines, we normally talked over the weekends.

We were managing our lives in a fairly decent manner. So, apparently everything was all well, which was actually not. He was totally unaware of what I was going through since last we met and even before that. It was no one's fault since I had acquired an art of faking happiness.

Next step I took immediately.

I called my husband on his phone. It was midnight at his place. I never called him that late. He became a bit worried due to the timing of my call. It was something urgent, he realized.

This time I didn't pretend that everything was 'all well' my side. I told him honestly about my mental health issue. First time, I cried while talking with him. I shared with him about my mental situation, my fearful status and dreadful anxiety issues. I made him aware how much depressed I was feeling and since how long. I simply wanted to cry that time.

I told him everything—what was making me cry, how lonely I was feeling all through that period of staying apart from each other, there was factually none to whom I could talk intimately or confidentially, my loneliness was haunting, it was killing me day by day, I was feeling as if it was no more me inside myself and I had lost the purpose of my life. I told him, I was feeling like being useless creature and rejected by others. Everything seemed like dejected, gloomy, useless to me. There was no excitement and happiness in life. I wanted perfection in my every task performed, which I was unable to do. I'd lost focus in life. I was getting dragged away from my goals and objectives in life. That was someone else whom I never knew, who was troubling me a great deal and I desperately wanted to be out of his clutches. I was going through suicidal ideations too often. He continued listening attentively.

I needed him very badly by my side to bring myself back to me, I stressed. I wanted to get cured of my depression and anxiety problems sooner possible, and in that resolve, I needed his help.

My husband listened to me attentively and compassionately without interrupting me. He kept the conversation confined to only about me and my problem. He played important role in consoling and comforting me that very juncture. He knew me as a bold person in normal situations and was able to manage my life affairs comfortably and could only sustain with self-support. I would never ask for any unwarranted assistance from him creating needless burden upon him. Hence, he comprehended the gravity of the situation. He realized that I was really in need of his help, the help which probably only he could offer to me and undoubtedly better than anyone else in that situation.

"Relax. Don't be panicky, dear. It can happen to anyone. Why didn't you tell me before? Don't worry. You're absolutely gonna be fine." My husband tried to calm down me.

"Stepping back from the problem would help clear your head. Eat well-balanced meals, sleep well and do your best. Instead of aiming for perfection, which isn't possible always, be proud of however close you get. Stay focused, stay away from distractions. Try to be happy and indulge in the activities you love to do." My husband advised.

"Be positive and stay optimistic. Remain mindful of your thoughts. Observe them, and let them go, trusting that God will work things out for you." He insisted.

Since he was in the middle of his contract period for his job, he was unable to get any leave for at least next 6-8 months. He took a very strong decision to support me, though, to be my side at that crucial juncture. He resigned from his job the very next day and decided to return to stay with me in next 10 days after submitting his resignation and completing all official formalities. It was indeed a tough decision, a very challenging one too, but for the love, safety and care of mine he preferred to opt for the choice of staying with me and leave his job.

At one point of time, I too felt embarrassing and uncomfortable to compel him to take such decision. However, he argued that life's precious, and I was more valuable to him than his job. I felt proud of him for his powerful thoughts and action.

"You are a fighter, you shall not give up, you will stumble, and you will fall but you will stand back up. It might take longer at times, but YOU WILL stand back up and keep fighting." By the time he got back with me, my husband kept encouraging me every day.

After 2 weeks, he was with me, constantly helping me in my resolve to bring back my original self.

I started working upon my much-needed lifestyle changes as per his guidance. I learnt the self-talk focusing upon strong optimism and positivity. Every day, I started performing physical exercises such as skipping rope and isometric workouts. Isometric muscle training moves helped me in improving my concentration and maintain my strength. Isotonic exercises helped me in providing physiological and physical benefits, such as increasing bone stress and overall energy and promoting weight loss.

I started getting less overwhelmed with my workload as I did before, and I just told myself that I can sit with these feelings and deal with them.

I thanked my husband for teaching me to accept my feelings and treat myself better than ever. I realized and agreed with those motivational thoughts which said that the dreams/nightmares are coming back because you are ready to deal with the abuse on a higher level.

"Let others lead small lives, but not you. Let others argue over small things, but not you. Let others cry over small hurts, but not you." -Jim Rohn. "If you can't fly then run, if you can't run then walk, if you can't walk then crawl, but whatever you do you have to keep moving forward." Martin Luther King Jr." Some of the greatest quotes of all time triggered me to push until something good happens. Forgetting what was behind me I got determined to strive to reach the goals ahead.

"Let me tell you something you already know. Life isn't all rainbows & sunshine. Life can beat you down on your knees & it will keep you there if you let it. There are also times when you're going to be beat down & you won't be able to move on. What matters is if you can take the hits & keep going. That's how winning is done. That's how champions are made. Finding meaning in life what you have got is the true spirit. Try to be harder and stronger. Good perseverance can overcome any difficulty in life." I learnt a lot while reading through the motivational sagas and life stories of illustrious people of the world.

These steps were a part of the framework that was going to make up my learning to live with my loss and plight. They were the tools to help me frame and identify what I was feeling and why. However big the problem is, life is certainly bigger than my problems, I comprehended. I was fully determined now.

CHAPTER 15

LIFE HAPPENS- APRIL 2016

When you are down, it's really hard to see any good in the world. People don't realize how much strength it takes to pull your own self out of a dark place mentally. Hence, when someone can do that, it would be the matter to feel good about. Consequently, when I could accomplish the same, I felt proud of myself.

All through those last 2-3 years, I'd tremendous feeling of being rejected by everyone. Especially at work. I wanted to bring perfection in my all work responsibilities, but unhealthy work environment, low motivation, low pay, job insecurity and lack of job satisfaction- all had compounded my problems. Moreover, being surrounded by low self-esteem, shirkers and frustrated people at work was making me more sick and tired. Deep inside, I was feeling low and battered. I also felt uncomfortable around others who didn't share similar interests with me or who didn't know me well enough and trying to judge me every so often.

Soon after my husband came back home, we planned a visit to our home country. I wanted to travel and write from my soul. I had plans. I wanted to meet old friends, make new friends and build my own business. I wanted to make it a new beginning for me. I really, really, really wanted to leave my gloomy last few years' time behind me and start with a new fresh chapter in my life. I desperately wanted to wake up every day excited to create my life, make my living and bring happiness, contentment, passion, and insight to other people and in turn, to myself. I wanted to speak on the causes I cared about in a perceptive, insightful, and persuasive way that influence others as much as I wanted to reunite the fragments of my own broken soul.

I was longing to meet my mother, my siblings, my friends and relatives whom I haven't seen in last many years due to my busy life. I wanted to spend good time with them, wanted to talk a lot and share beautiful nostalgic moments with them to revive my happiness and interest in life. It was much needed to revitalize my dead self. I was reinventing myself. I was determined to feel the life now. I wanted to realize my worth at that juncture after dwelling through the days, months and couple of years of distress and feelings of futility and incompetence. I wanted to be at those places where I'd achieved best professional positions and enjoyed best part of my life.

My husband and I decided to spend a month's period in touring various places and revive nostalgic memories. My husband believed that travel would enhance my mental well-being. I would definitely feel good, I also agreed. I wanted to pursue a life on road, travelling would make me a happier person by building self-confidence, providing new experiences and memories, I was pretty excited about our whole travel program and meeting people.

I still had professional association with one of the international universities. Hence, I took that opportunity to visit the university where I taught few years ago during my academic career. After landing, I decided to visit the university very next day. I was very eager to meet people there, reviving my memories.

After landing, the next day, I visited my department of psychiatry where once I worked as the head of the department. I met the teaching and administrative staff there. The ongoing batches of the students were excited to see me. There were few old students too who were now working as lecturers, assistant professors, or professors in various departments. All greeted me with love, affection, respect and gratitude. It was heartwarming to see the professional growth and progress of my old students. They gave credit for their success and growth to my constant support and guidance I provided them during their studentship. Their compliments and true affection brought tears of humility and contentment in my eyes.

I felt truly honored and humbled by their kind words and generous gestures. It was a great experience for me. I instantaneously realized what I was missing in my life, by now!

It is so supporting and meaningful to hear that what we did something was good or that who we are is being valued. We are social animals. As human beings, we long for connection, for sure. It gives great feeling when someone respects us, recognizes and appreciates our integrity, our thoughtfulness, caring, knowledge, or compassion. We feel good when a person recognizes qualities that we appreciate about ourselves. It feels good to be seen and being appreciated for what we do to others. It also helps satisfy our yearning for healthy relationships. In true sense, it strengthens a perception of meaning in our lives.

The nostalgic memories and affection of the people of that place made me regain my lost confidence. I instantly felt like being loved, appreciated and important to others. Everyone was excited to meet me and discuss professional matters with me. I was like feeling high and my brain seemed to be releasing dopamine, phenylethylamine and oxytocin all together! In that moment, I realized that my people had valued and noticed me amidst my fast-paced life and embraced me with their full committed love and respect. I could see, I'd been treasured and still cherished!

I was elated to see that I'd touched their lives and made a difference in their lives. Now, they were doing the same to me, oblivious to what actually I was going through at that point of time and which was much needed at that juncture in my life!

I stayed there for couple of weeks. I was offered an honorary teaching position in my department for about 4 weeks period. I immediately accepted the offer with pleasure and started working enthusiastically in my department in the same way as I once did.

I was very happy and excited. I noticed I was absolutely in control of myself during that time. I was enthusiastic to teach the new batches of students and help them in their preclinical and clinical studies through various assignments and practicals. I was discussing various case reports and topics for the thesis for the department's post grad students! I was sitting in the same chair when I worked as Head of the Department few years ago, which in fact did boost my esteem and morals. It was a proud moment for me! I was totally elated and in highest spirit. This was real me! I told myself.

"Look at yourself, you're the same person, nothing has changed, dear!" my inner self told me cheerfully!

CHAPTER 16

JULY 2016

When I returned from India to Toronto after spending few productive weeks enriched with professional and personal gains, I was feeling a lot more relaxed, blissful and rejuvenated. I felt I was yet not ready to bounce back with full vigor and verve to achieve my desired goal in life, though. For the most part, I was cheerful and revived one; yet it was like half the battle had been won. My struggle with my inner demons, nonetheless, was not over fully. My demons were trying to return to me intermittently and eager to push me into darkness and gloom whenever I experienced a low spirit. My negativity too was trying to recapture my mind every so often. I'd understood the wicked game of my demons, however.

The process of my revival would be gradual and challenging, I was aware of, right from the beginning of my resolve to get cured. I'd gathered myself by that time, though. Consequently, I wanted to give myself some more time to be fully prepared before embarking upon journey to the next level in my life. I kept constantly motivating, encouraging and gearing up myself to greet the upcoming new life by reminding 'The Best is Coming, Dear!'

The next significant step before embracing the new phase of my life I took was to plan another expedition. I wanted to travel to the places I always desired to see in my life and relax a bit. My husband and I planned a small trip to world's most beautiful, historical places. We travelled to Europe. Greece, Italy, UK and Spain, my favorite places. We visited Athens in Greece and Rome in Italy first followed by Vatican City, Italy, London in UK, Paris in France and Barcelona in Spain. We spent a nearly 4 weeks' period travelling different places in various cities.

During our expedition, we met many travelers and shared various delightful travelling experiences with them. We also met local people and enjoyed local delicacies with them. We also took road trips across the country stopping at different National Parks, historical sites and anything else that looked intriguing to us along the way. It was an amazing experience for us. We were very excited and open to new opportunities, experiences and interactions to truly absorb cultural diversities and feel of the place. We were happy to meet like-minded travelers who introduced us to new experiences they've discovered during their travel. We'd eternally feel connected to them because they're the only ones who would comprehend the experiences we shared in new environment, I strongly felt that very point of time.

In Athens, Rome and Barcelona we spent few of the most beautiful moments of my life. In Athens, we visited the main attractions- The Acropolis, the Temple of Olympian Zeus, and the Ancient Agora. They were incredible and interesting; I was feeling excited. Athens has most significant ancient monuments in the world- the Acropolis, greatest museum-The National Archaeological Museum, which houses most important finds from Greece's Archaeological Sites and others. I loved all so much. Athens' glory days occurred much earlier in history that Rome's did, so it seemed liked its buildings were unscathed by the passing of time! Rome too amazed me, captivated me for long time. Coming to Rome and Athens, I'd thought the two cities would be very similar since Roman Empire was heavily influenced by Greek culture. It was true. I visited Colosseum-an epic monument to the gladiatorial battles, The Pantheon, Capitoline, Trevi Fountain etc. in Rome. In Spain, I visited beautiful Barcelona, The Sagrada Familia, Las Ramblas, and Marvel at Santa Maria del Mar etc. I enjoyed visiting Buckingham Palace, London Eye, Tower Bridge, etc. in London, and Eiffel Tower, Mont Arc de Triomphe, and the Notre-Dame Cathedral in France.

The effect of traveling and exploring all those wonderful places was instantaneous. There's a whole world out there, I was so happy. Life was meant for great adventures and close friends; I realized the essence of life. The valor of the great fighters of that time and the great personalities imbibed in me values of life, how they fought against all odds in their lives and made great achievements became a great inspiration for me. My visit to Europe taught me a few things about life and helped me come up with "rules" that I tried to implement in my daily routine thereon like:

Don't be quick to judge, even if it is about your own life incidents, since you don't know really what is good and bad for you.

Don't compare. Each experience is unique and incredible in its own way. By comparing one incident to another you won't be able to appreciate the result for what it was- to enjoy or to learn. Every experience, however, brings you a level of understanding and a level of maturity, for sure.

Keep your expectations in check. High expectations can lead to disappointment. There is nothing wrong with expecting every day and every event to be the best and most amazing time, nevertheless, good to try and refrain from having very lofty and specific expectations so that you don't feel too let down if the outcome doesn't live up to our imagination.

Don't dwell on what you can't control. Getting worked up about things that are out of your hands will only bring negativity to your life. Try to enjoy every moment, however, if that's not possible, feel every moment since its precious gift of Almighty and comes to you to serve a definite purpose in your life. Positive psychology encourages us focus on the positive things in life, though, without denying the negative side of life.

Upon return from my much-cherished sabbatical, I felt really refreshed and rejuvenated. I felt that vacation indeed helped my life perceptions to change a lot from negative to positive. My thought processes were transformed from pessimism to optimism. I was focused and oriented towards my goals and my life now. I committed myself to reading and writing motivational and personal development write-ups to encourage myself. I started talking with myself, singing and dancing for me. Life, no doubt, had been very complex and messy during all that time. But motivation was something that I learnt to create at will from my experience. Becoming deeply passionate could also be within our creative control. As a result, we can completely predict our own success, I felt. We can choose to become as successful as we want, defying all challenges, I convinced myself. The motivational and spiritual write ups which I read and wrote during that phase of my life led me through the therapy process and helped me stay engaged. I made a habit of recording things I was thankful for each day. I took the time to feel and enjoy the moments when any of my senses were delighted.

Our trip energized me to full extent. I was determined to bounce back with all of my energy and strength in life. I was all set now. We had the best holidays of our life, for sure. I was feeling like completely enlightened. My husband and I were totally refreshed and recharged for our new venture in life which we started executing as per our plan soon after reaching home.

I could remember now that my period of anxiety which used to last 1-2 weeks originally, totally exhausting me ending with depression, had reduced to a significant level. Although, I wasn't fully normal, the things were changing drastically now-in my favor! I saw a definite transformation in me. It had been a couple of months; I was feeling better-mentally and physically. My regular physical exercises, yoga, meditation practices were going on smoothly. My husband and my dog were providing constant support and healing touch to me during that period of my recovery. They were my assets and my energy; I was thankful to Almighty for the same. I was feeling warmth and liveliness in my life were gradually restoring back.

One fine day while I was sitting in meditation, I felt something totally different. It was unlike any other day. Suddenly I realized I hadn't been significantly anxious in last few months. I was free! These were really good news for me! I strongly felt I was out of the clutches of my demons! Gone were the days when I was under the solid influence of depression and anxiety- fear of flying to self-doubt, sleepless nights, agonizing days and panic attacks were gone! I was completely a new person now, a normal person- with normal feelings, attitudes and actions. I was looking at my rejuvenated self from outside and cherishing my new form. It was my inner joy, happiness and strength to be normal. I was strongly feeling the eternal bliss in my life. My God was more powerful than my demons, it was proved without any doubt. I'd never felt so encouraged and empowered to tackle something so challenging in my life. It was really an amazing feeling to see your original self-returning in the pure form after so long time of mental and physical struggles!

I criticized and scolded myself often, before. However, my self-talk was now gentle and thoughtful. I wasn't continuously haunted by my problems anymore; I'd tackled them by acknowledging and addressing them slowly but surely. It took me a lot to get to that point, for sure, but the reward was well worth the effort.

CHAPTER 17

March 2017

In January 2017, I and my husband started a business at a prominent location in GTA. I started working as a Director in our own business. It was a new venture for us. My husband and I both were pretty excited about our new enterprise in our lives. It was a challenging endeavor, though. It was a project involving high investment of money, time, energy, efforts and hard work. It also required tenacity and grit, dedication and resolve to perform in the best of our capacities. We were determined, nevertheless, to do something great for our lives, in our own way.

In last few years, I was totally fed up with my life and the work I was doing. I wanted to do something very exciting and challenging yet satisfying now. However, I wasn't very clear in my mind exactly what to do. I wasn't sure how planning something on my own would work out? What if I fail?! That was a hidden fear. Despite all dilemma, I was very much convinced for what not to do at that very juncture. I didn't want to join the same institution where I worked before my expedition. I'd already resigned from the position and had decided never to go back to the same people again. Also, I'd decided to never work on the same job position with similar conditions and going through the same hell which I'd gone through in last few years! I'd realized the essence of life. Each passing day was valuable for me and I was determined to make it very meaningful henceforth.

My ambitions were very much alive and kicking steadfastly notwithstanding my traumatic past with my lost vigor and vitality. I wanted to be happy hereafter, and work and live happily for rest of my life. I didn't want to do anything which may be the cause for relapse of my condition, though. I'd already been through the hell, and there was no guarantee not to be revisited by the same demons if the things go wrong in life! I'd to be very cautious and vigil, I forewarned myself.

I was experiencing a great sense of relief and freedom after resigning from my previous job. I was so much happy for my decision that very point of time and never regretted ever. I'm very happy and content about my decision even now and will always be so. On the contrary, I am living with the grudge that why did I take so long to act prudently? I could have opted for the same much earlier. I'd wasted important part of my life doing unpleasant things and tortured myself.

Anyway, when I took the decision to work for our own self and not for others, my husband supported me in my decision about starting this new education business enterprise. He helped me in its execution as well. This idea was my brainchild. It was like my dream come true to be self-employed and have the freedom to plan and execute novel ideas for our own enterprise. My basic objectives for being self-employed were control over all business aspects, use of my knowledge and skills in most appropriate manners, without any interference from others, and of course, increased earning potential. There were other benefits such as job security, flexibility in my work routine and job satisfaction leading to an improved quality of life as well. What else a workaholic and passionate person such as me look forward to? Thus, the business happened to us and I became an entrepreneur!

I heard once an industry mogul advising a business starter that he would have to take deep breath as before jumping off the entrepreneurial cliff and finally going for the ride. His ride could be like a rollercoaster- with huge ups and correspondingly scary downs. So, he would need to be patient and persistent to be successful. I knew the rollercoaster ride symbolizes the ups and downs of life. It teaches you the fundamentals of life. It teaches you that not all time remains same, time changes so quick. So, keep working, stay focused and oriented. In business, you need to be courageous. 'Don't be the person who's too fearful to jump off the entrepreneurial cliff,' I encouraged myself.

It was a new, invigorated life. I was feeling like a fresh breeze. I was totally new to all intricacies related to a private business enterprise, though. I and my husband had lot of practical knowledge and experience in academics and administrative fields, per se. Until now, we were working for others and utilizing our expertise and skills for others, though. We worked hard for others and provided abundant ideas to others, which worked perfectly for them and made them thrive. Now, we wanted to serve our selves and were happy for that matter. We'd total freedom to execute our ideas and had great plans.

I've been a big believer of just-in-time learning per se. With a curious mind, I kept my eyes and ears open for new ideas. Before starting our venture, I studied thoroughly about business complexities and strategies. The first step in a successful business enterprise would be- the Desire, then the Idea, then the plan and then the execution. I learnt. I was in a ready mode.

 'If you are not scared, then your goals are not big enough. Reach for the sky and when you reach your goal, set another one- bigger and bolder.' I constantly kept stimulating myself.

CHAPTER 18

January 2020

My husband and I worked very hard, day and night to make our business first work and then succeed. Ours was a small business, but our dreams and goals were super high. We tried every bit to make our dream successful. Our dream was our child, and we were nurturing with it with all our love, care, sweat, hard work and passion. We focused on quality customer service. While keeping ego in check, we listened every customer and got feedback from others and kept improving. We always responded promptly to voicemails or emails from customers. We constantly kept expanding our marketing efforts, built our online presence and updated our business plan accordingly.

Amidst very hectic and demanding professional life, we tried to find an acceptable level of work-life balance, stay healthy and allow us and our business to prosper over the long term. We stayed balanced and kept working year by year with the resolve to make each year better than the previous one.

It'd been nearly 4 years since we sow the seeds in our minds of running our own business and become self-employed. Life is much smoother and of better quality for us now. We are happy, content and enthusiastic every day for what we are doing. We are working hard, and dividend of our hard work is paying off. We've learned a lot with passing time, and we will continue to keep learning as we grow.

'When you're determined, even God helps you to fulfill your dream.' I'm a great believer of this. I strongly feel a continuous source of positive energy radiating out from my body and mind every time when I implement a new idea in my work, irrespective of its outcome. I am confident about my strength, skills and capabilities. I stay positive about the things, in general, nevertheless, negative developments don't depress me much now since my positive frame of mind and positive energy keep counteracting the negativity at every level in my life.

Life has come a long way since my *anxiety and depression* days.

Now with my anxiety and depression under my control, my heart has got filled with the feelings of delight and gratitude. Happiness sometimes just creeps in, and when I feel I've received it, it's like a gift of destiny helping me fully embrace self-love and self-acceptance. As someone who once lived every moment in an emotional torment and distraught, I appreciate feelings of eternal peace and satiation. There's a joy of existence inside the serenity of my heart.

I can't overlook that I was 49 when I'd an anxiety attack that was so severe that it threw me into a mental breakdown, followed by a sad, dark period of depression. I was crying myself to sleep every night and never saw any hope to recover from that dark period. However, out of that event I was really able to get the insight of my mental health and ever since have been able to stay in a good way and not slip back into the cycle that I'd been going through for so long.

As I became aware that my thoughts were the predominant cause of my anxiety, not necessarily every situation at hand, I started ignoring the patterns of thinking that seemed to be the catalyst for such episodes. I feel that anxiety and depression are connected to distorted thinking patterns, whether they are worries about the future or dwelling on a past event or related to PTSD. Moreover, the overthinking about inevitable or uncontrollable eventualities of life can be negative and fearful and generates stress and anxiety which may lead to depression. Hence, developing ability to recognize these patterns of thinking as the trigger for anxiety and depression is incredibly powerful achievement. It indeed worked for me. Now, whenever I feel an episode of anxiety approaching me, I simply know that my thinking is out of whack.

Presently, I am a very busy individual with my work routine and daily life. I enjoy my work. I work nearly 12-13 hours in a typical weekday in my office and then at home. I often work on weekends too, nearly same hours as on weekdays. Despite working for long hours and hard work, I feel more energetic and enthusiastic compared to few years ago. I am happy and content for what I am doing. I am optimistic for my future as well. I am not very worried about the future and don't keep extremely high expectations, though.

I simply try and stay present, stay in the here and the now. I try to disconnect completely from my thoughts as soon as they try to concentrate on negativity. I've realized that- one can't completely avoid mild to moderate anxiety in routine life. However, we can overcome dreadful overpowering of our minds by anxiety and depression once we identify them and develop resolve to fight back full throttle. It was an easier said than done initially, but every time I did it and still am doing it, I feel my anxiety slowly dissipates and eventually subsides. Whereas in the past I would mull over the thoughts in my head which would drive the anxiety up further and eventually throw me into a state of depression.

My work keeps me lively and serves as an incessant source of energy booster. Happiness at work is the feeling that I really enjoy what I do, and I am proud of myself.

CHAPTER 19

May 2020- Covid-19 Ruling
the Crazy World

It's 10.30 am on Wednesday in May month- usually a very busy time of day and month. While standing near the window, what I see outside is deserted streets and what I hear is pin drop silence. The roads are empty, with most people staying home. Needless to say, I'm home. It's been more than a month; I'm working from my home. The people in my neighborhood too are following 'Social or Physical Distancing' and 'Stay home' guidelines imposed by the government and health authorities plainly. Thanks to Corona virus pandemic, the whole world has turned upside down in last few months. What we are seeing and living in the world today, none of us have had ever thought of in the wildest dream! WHO, the governments, health authorities and people- all are geared up globally to deal with the effects and consequences of corona virus pandemic. No specific treatment, medication or vaccine is available so far to cure this devastating infection, though.

Few months back no one heard and cared about the corona virus. In last 3-4 months world over 1 million people have been infected and over 100,000 deaths have occurred due to corona. Until now, coronavirus COVID-19 has affected at least 210 countries and territories around world. As news about the coronavirus outbreak continues to dominate the headlines and millions of people globally, we have been sternly asked to self-quarantine and stay home. Scientists have even warned we may need to live with social distancing for few months or a year or more. Nothing is actually predictable about corona pandemic, how far it will go and how much devastating it will be! In the wake of this pandemic, as per researchers we've two scary choices: practice social distancing for months or a year or let hundreds of thousands die. It seems that the ongoing battle with corona virus is a long-lasting process and certainly not going to end very soon, despite of our want and need to do so. It's a frightening fact, enough to disturb mental balance of many on the global arena. Lots of anxiety, depression and fear are gripping all minds.

Owing to stay home and social distancing measures, most people are compelled to spend most of their time at home and making us deprived of their regular activities and lifestyle. Closed environment of four walls often induce feelings of claustrophobia (fear of confined place) and cleithrophobia (fear of being trapped). Working from home may not be a practicable option for all. Corona pandemic has displaced many lives as a whole. Global panic over corona virus pandemic is attributed to significant factors such as crushed global economy, broken healthcare systems, projected food shortage, widespread infection and mortality, political damage, worldwide recession and post-corona situation, to list a few. We're in midst of a worldwide pandemic, with cities and countries shutting down. No one is sure for what is in store in future! This uncertainty surrounding corona virus is the hardest to handle. The plight and predicaments due to corona pandemic has started causing mental health issues for significant population globally. It's challenging to navigate this uncertainty, social separation and fear psychosis. Hence, in the face of this unique crisis, it's very vital to manage our anxiety, fears, depression and stress and maintain mental health along with physical health. I've managed to maintain my mental health by following some coping strategies, however. I am constantly calming myself by following advices:

a. Don't panic. Be pragmatic and aware about the facts of this crisis and behave rationally. Avoid the misguiding news and messages. Read, listen, convey the facts. Facts will help reduce fears.

b. While realizing worth of physical distancing, keep in touch with friends using technology.

c. Stay happy, busy and active. Do joyous activities and avoid sad, gloomy and negativity. Reinventing myself by indulging in my favorite hobbies of singing, and gardening during this pandemic. Creativity helped me reduce my anxiety, depression, and stress during this crisis.

I have realized by this time that coronavirus pandemic is not only testing our capacity, patience and perseverance but also checking competence of world's strongest healthcare services. It's a learning lesson for everyone on this earth. A tiny virus has exhibited its tremendous power to shake the whole world and we all are compelled to be united in this battle against virus, as a blessing in disguise!

I'm constantly advising others around me too that we're experiencing a different kind of period in our life; it need not be bad one, though. Corona Virus Pandemic is bringing out the best and worst of all of us. We all need to protect ourselves and community by staying home and helping each other by physical distancing. However, stress, anxiety, depression or fear due to social isolation must not dampen our spirit to fight against corona pandemic. We are all together in this fight. Be positive, patient, aware and follow healthcare guidelines strictly- must be our mantra for successfully fight corona virus pandemic.

My message in this time of crisis is simple and clear- Nothing last forever. This crisis will get over one day. Be positive, be patient and behave sensibly and thoughtfully till then. Help the needy while protecting yourself. Tough time doesn't last, but tough people will!

CHAPTER 20

DECEMBER 2020- VICTORY
OVER THE EVIL-DEVIL

My life has come a long way since my 'anxiety' days. I feel more like original 'ME' with lively attitude. I've boarded the flight of life again with full vigor, verve, vitality and vengeance. Despite the constant fear and threat of COVID-19, I am not afraid of anxiety or depression since I feel they're the distorted patterns of thinking and identification with the thoughts that we start believing to be true. I feel like I've understood the mental health as a patient and know how to deal with. As soon as I become disconnected from them and cognizant of what is transpiring, I get free from the cycle of anxiety-depression-anxiety that caused me immense suffering for last few years, disturbing my happy life and loss of confidence.

Clinically diagnosed anxiety is not just being a little worried or concerned. It eats into our wellbeing, confidence, health and life, and it's a continuous process- prevailing 24x7. Even at work every passing comment feels a negative remark. We constantly do more to get over the feeling that we ain't good enough and strive to prove ourselves. The exhaustion from not sleeping because we agonize and panic all night over what we can't influence or failed to prove ourselves drives us crazy. Persistent insomnia and stress take a toll on our physical and mental health. We make mistakes, we start living in a fog, and it becomes a vicious circle.

I think a lot of people's anxiety and/or depression is caused by negative thinking or traumatic or untoward event-past or present. Those suffering from medical issues need to get good professional advice and support. I realized with self-help and positive thinking that I could take control of my own thinking patterns and over time turn a mindset of depression into calmness and happiness. The task may not seem very easy, but not impossible either.

I do agree, different people are suffering from different types of mental illness and there's no *one size fits all* approach when it comes to alleviating the suffering of an individual. However, by talking to people and discussing all benefit from mutual experiences and knowledge. Awareness of our own problems enables us to gain clarity and understanding about what we are dealing with. That makes us able to take practical steps to regain control of our mental state. The steps may be customized to suit individual needs and requirements.

If I hadn't been through these things, I wouldn't have learnt that the most important thing in life is to BE HAPPY. I've now increased interest in all my activities, and I can now see a bright future for me. I hope to live my life with a definite perspective, I am doing the work and things that I love, something that makes ME happy, not focusing upon what others want from me. I am totally oriented for my inner peace, pleasure while perceiving my passion in the profession I love. The best part of my life is- I am able to do what I love and yet when that's not possible, I love what I do. Life becomes much easier by his approach, I've realized.

When I started my educational business, I had intentions of earning money enough to live life comfortably and have job satisfaction to set me free from the rat race I was once living. And now I am able to run the same successfully with great self-respect, raised self-esteem and job satisfaction.

Top of all, I am really happy that I am touching the life of many people every day while serving them through right education for their successful professional life, and that gives me tremendous sense of pride and privilege. I'm above an average everyday individual trying to better myself and my internal and external strength each passing day so I can give myself the life I ever dreamt of and I deserve.

I would love to help out wherever I can, I think some of my experiences can definitely benefit others as I know exactly what they are going through and understand how deliberating these conditions can be.

CHAPTER 21

INSIGHT

Mental Health Awareness is a critical subject matter which needs to be understood thoroughly. I've learnt a lot from my anxiety and depression. Here is some of the important insight that I acquired from my experience, would like to share with all. I hope all those fighting any of these demons may find this information of some worth to understand and value the mental health.

In the past few years according to global surveys and studies it has been estimated that one in six people have experienced an issue with their mental health. Anxiety and depression harm and destroy affected individuals in diverse ways. Many do suffer from social anxiety disorder (SAD), which is characterized by a consistent and disproportionate fear of social situations resulting in avoidance of, or intense discomfort in, such situations. Mental health issues—most commonly depression, anxiety, stress and drug use —are some of the main causes of the global concern.

Mental health is as much significant as physical health of an individual. It is not your heart, but your mind, which could be a real troublemaker for you. Your mind is stronger than your heart to give you inconceivable troubles. You become what you constantly think and believe. Your mind makes you to think that way. It's your mind and your thought processes which you need to pay attention to while facing anxiety challenges.

Someone physically fit and perfect can be incredibly sick due to mental health problems. If it is you, admit it, understand it and try to focus upon going back to your normal self rather than succumbing to the evil effects of the disorder. Remember, medicines may not be a perfect remedy for you, if you don't strengthen yourself to defy the challenges you've been put into. It is only you, who can and will help yourself!

However big problem may be, Life is certainly bigger than it. Love your life, respect and value your life. The struggle with all that pain, agonies, sorrow, your heart will fix itself. It is your mind; you need to worry about. Your mind where you've locked memories- good or bad, stored the pieces of the ones that- hurt you, insulted you, harmed you- that still cut you like razor. Your mind has the capacity to keep you up at night, make you cry, feel self-pity, destroy you over and over again.

You need to convince your mind that it has to let go, because your heart already knows how to heal it. When our mind is constantly wandering, it signifies that we're subliminally dissatisfied with our presence and life.

The journey of my life from the year 2011 to year 2015 was awful. It was turbulent and full of emotional and physical upheavals. There were more lows than high tides and I was drifting with tides. I constantly felt I've been to hell and back. I'd lost confidence about my abilities and doubting every move of mine. I was depressed and frustrated too. When I talk about my present than I would say this doesn't mean that depression is a terrific thing having only negative values because it definitely isn't, but I believe you must turn your negative experiences into positive ones if you can.

The best of life can come from the worst of life! There is nothing like a perfect life. There's nothing wrong in admitting your weakness, fears and failures. The person who can bring out the best in you and make you strong, is actually your weakness!

Although good preaching advices to be happy in every situation, you can't be all the time, per se. Being a human, you've certain emotions. If you feel like defeated, admit it. If you feel like traumatized, admit it. If you feel like lost, admit it. There is nothing wrong. If you feel like broken and devastated, share it with close one, try to find out the solution for your problem with joint efforts. However, strengthen yourself. Make promise to be strong to yourself and behave like the same because you're the best person to share with all your good and bad in life.

When we don't know how to control our sentimentalism and emotional responses, and just let them linger for hours or days, it turns into an attitude. There's a refractory period for recovery. If we keep that refractory period going on for weeks and months and don't recover, we will grow into a character. If we keep that same refractory period going on for years, it's called a personality trait. Disbelief, negativity, skepticism, and scorn can become our character traits this way. This is a terrible and unproductive way to live life.

However great person one may be, they always have some flows in life, and everyone requires counseling at one point of time. I don't know anyone fully engaged in human life who doesn't face a personal demon here and there. Most of us face a lot of them. It certainly takes an unyielding amalgamation of self-determination, resolve, tenacity and spiritual fortitude to face your inner fears, battle your personal anxiety, battle your PTSD, and fight personal demons successfully. We all have the capacity to sustain in every situation and hence, must aspire to find joy in all small things in life. Anyone can have a mental health problem. But unfortunately, we don't know what to do or what to say or how exactly required to behave with them. It's more important to respond sensitively to someone who seems troubled than to find out fault in his/her behavior and be judgmental. We may never know what they may be going through. We must be also sympathetic and empathetic to such individuals. Be ready to reach out to them and help.

It is really imperative you don't minimize the other person's feelings any way in a manner that may put them in further vulnerable position, which many people can do without realizing. Sometimes, by trying to give advice or be helpful, the friends and family of someone with a mental health problem can do more harm than good.

When someone cancels, or ducks out, or makes a contemptible excuse, please understand that it may not be intentional. It may not be personal, out of idleness or procrastination. Please understand that they are not being rude or disrespectful to you. It's simply because they can't physically do it, can't mentally handle it. When someone needs supporting/encouraging/ hand holding it isn't absurd. It isn't immaturity or goofing off, it's because they are desperate to beat it but can't do it alone. They need your attention, your help, your support and your assistance to come out of that brain fog, foggy headedness created by anxiety muddled mind. It's difficult to understand how tiring it is to act ok and look strong when in reality you're close to the edge.

It is not obligatory always that only your doctor can provide you with the solution to your problem. Most of the time sufferers fall prey to medications trap as well. They only rely upon drugs to stay active and alive, oblivious to the awful fact that drugs may do more harm to you than good, at times. They become drug dependents and may be later on drug addicts. Most of them lose the resolve to get cured, per se. I've seen many people known to me who fell prey to paradoxic effects of the drugs they took for their psychotic disorders, anxiety or depression, stress or schizophrenia. These individuals, unfortunately, have lost vision in their life. They are unmotivated and pessimistic about their life and have lost faith in themselves. They keep suffering in silence and don't share their problems with others, which they must do to benefit in such situation. Your friends, families, professional help and support system may come to your rescue in such situations and can help you a great deal to come out of crisis fruitfully. Nevertheless, it's very vital to know that if you don't help yourself, none will and can help you.

'Best help comes from self' I trust. God also helps those who want to help themselves, I believe. You're your best friend and your best motivator; don't underestimate the power of your companionship with yourself. Many times, you've the capacity to find solution of your problem yourself, provided you pay attention to your inner voice and identify your strengths and weaknesses. Unfortunately, in the time of crisis, minds remain shut; they lose their power to think rationally. Even wisest individuals may lose their vision in the event of catastrophe. If that happens with you, don't get amazed. It's very usual. It's very natural. Just try to remain positive and calm. If good time didn't last, the bad time won't either, for sure! New beginning is always waiting for you—don't forget the pleasant fact.

You travel in the time zone when you may have always thought about others until now. Now, it is all about YOU. You must realize that an investment in yourself will earn the best interest. Don't run away from yourself, which is a very peculiar phenomena generally found with the sufferers of severe stress, anxiety, depression or schizophrenia like psychological conditions. I know it very much since I'd been there and seen all. I've had observed myself from a very close quarter experiencing diverse kinds of feelings pertaining to self-rejection, self-denial, loss of self-esteem and self-hate. Trust yourself, love yourself and listen to yourself.

Anxiety kills, Depression kills, PTSD kills, Stress kills, Tension kills, Negativity kills. Stay optimistic if you can't be vivacious and passionate all the time. Universal words of wisdom say—

'stay always happy and cheerful'. In practical life that's not always feasible, though. No worries. Don't lose your confidence —it's the bottom-line. Feel the feelings. Feel the things and happenings in and around you. Stay away from the negative people and negative energy, however. They kill you eternally. The most successful thing and people on the earth are—Negativity and negative minded people, in my view; whom I always found working in their best abilities and getting success very easily and never loose initial battle, especially when the prey is weak-minded and vulnerable.

A negative attitude is worse than a cancerous growth, I believe. Everyone has at least one difficult trial in life, yes, everyone. So, be strong and stay positive. You can kill all negativity with divinity and positivity. Have faith in yourself. Have faith in your faith (divine faith). I do believe in spirituality. For me, spirituality is a broad concept with place for many perspectives, per se. In general, it includes a sense of connection to something bigger than us. It typically entails a search for a meaningful life. As such, it is a universal human experience—something that touches us all.

The spiritual aspect of our life implies to spiritual energy working at a deep level upon us to provide eternal healing. The healing comprises the transfer of energy. It does not come from the healer himself or herself, but the healer links with Universal energy or Divine energy to focus upon the healing for the mind, body and spirit.

I firmly believe my own energy and divine energy-both worked appreciably for my healing processes and helped me recover without any further damage to me-physically, psychologically and morally. I can't be more thankful for that!

CHAPTER 22

KEY AREAS NEEDING
YOUR ATTENTION

Staying alone/Isolation/Family Support

Staying alone and away from family, friends or group of people is not good when you are passing through severe stress or mental sickness. Staying alone when you are feeling lonely and deprived, is detrimental to your mental and physical health. It makes you vulnerable for many life problems since you are morally and emotionally may not be strong enough. Avoid staying alone since it also increases your loneliness and makes you prone to many undesirable consequences such as suicidal ideation or criminal activity too.

Sometimes a release is exactly what we need when we are lonely or under severe stress or anxiety. Different people exhibit this release in different ways. Some people cry angry tears to vent their anger, hopelessness or frustrations. It's a way that we've developed to soothe ourselves in tough situations. We cry when we're lonely and sad. Crying is a healthy emotional response. Anger and frustration are intense emotions, which can produce the same physiological reaction. Sometimes just saying out loud that you ain't OK can feel like a huge release in itself. Acknowledging how you are feeling without judging yourself is one of the important methods to help yourself. More you pretend to be OK, more troubled and fake you feel to yourself.

Not all the time crying, or venting frustration can be good practice for release, though. Often using mental grounding techniques to calm your emotions prove to be very helpful. Talk about your anger with the people involved in the situation. Perhaps it would be beneficial for you to reach out to someone that you trust and talk to them about how you feel. This can be highly therapeutic. Talking to someone is one of the best ways to overcome your anxiety. Getting together with your family and friends, even your colleagues at workplace, and talking about your feelings can be helpful. Best support you may get it from your family and best friends, who understand you well and would always be ready to help you. Hence, never hide your feelings and tribulations from them. They are the real gems which would shine brightly in your darkness to help you get rid of all your worries and anxiety.

If you feel shy about your plight or can't talk to someone, try writing a letter/e-mail or online chat room to discuss about your condition and seek help. Nowadays, there's a whole section of society including medical experts, psychologists, health professionals, community health services and mental health organizations ready to help 24x7. Don't feel ashamed of your condition. Nothing wrong in giving yourself time and opportunity to heal. Seal your painful wounds which are bleeding every day and troubling you before they get necrosed. Prevent any further damage and relapse, it's in your hands. Learn to say firm, loud and clear 'NO' to demons of depression and anxiety, hovering above your mind and ready to strike you.

Remember-You have all the rights to get love from others the way you deserved to be loved, for that matter you have to love yourself first. Start loving back yourself from this very moment. Keep your moral high. Talk to the people—known or unknown too. Simple "Hello", "Hi" "Thank you" to everyone may help you open up. Regular exchange of open-ended questions with people around you such as "How are you", "How was your day" or "What are your hobbies?" are excellent starters for brief and long conversations and mood changes.

Staying in the company of positive minded, vibrant, happy, vivacious people will certainly do the trick. It's good for our immune system and mental health to nurture the positive sense of connection with optimistic and positive thought processes that can come from communicating and interacting with such people. Keep yourself busy doing the things you always enjoyed the most when you felt normal. The best way to avoid grumpiness and bad temper is to remain happy and for that matter company of happy people is a necessity.

Hormones and mental health

Hormones share close-knit relation with a person's mental health. Anxiety due to hormonal imbalance is caused by an imbalance in the endocrine system. Hormonal imbalance can occur at various age and stage in life. Although hormonal imbalance and its consequences are observed to be more pronounced in women, it can affect both-men and women in various conditions.

Menopause in women- Approaching middle age itself brings increased stress, anxiety, and fear. Changing hormone levels during perimenopause and menopause can affect your physical and emotional health. Perimenopause is the phase before the final menstrual period during which the body undergoes many physical changes. Some women have acute feelings of anxiety or panic attacks during perimenopause too. During menopause, rapid drop in estrogen and progesterone leads to mood changes, hot flashes, sweating, irritability, anxiety, restlessness, agitation, frustration and angry outbursts. There come the feelings of guilt or worthlessness, trouble concentrating or making decisions, loss of interest in activities you used to enjoy, too little or too much sleep, weird physical pain, forgetfulness, fatigue, changes in your appetite too name a few.

Male menopause-refers to hormonal changes that some men experience as they get older due to decrease in testosterone levels leading to variety of symptoms and complications such as erectile dysfunction, obesity and fatigue. When this hormonal system gets out of balance, symptoms of anxiety, depression, irritability, mood swings, foggy brain, tense muscles, and sleep disturbances can occur, leading to the partial to total disturbance in daily routine with life thrown out of gear.

In general, women suffer more from anxiety than men and at menopause. There may also be emotional changes, such as worries about getting older, losing family members, or children leaving home. These factors play great role in your daily happiness or contentment. The very sense of security and feelings of being loved by your family and friends give you impetus to live and enjoy your life. When your family or children leave you and you're left alone at home-it provides you instant creepy feeling-a sense of desertion, dejection and estrangement. One can realize the value of love, care, safety and security of a well-knit family, when they don't have them or have lost them.

Through my own experience, I learnt that women may have to tackle their issues in various conditions. For many women, menopause may be a time of isolation or frustration. At times, family and friends may also not understand what you're going through or give you the support you actually require. It's hard to find empathy from others for many during this time of physical and mental struggle of coping with the situation and it's possible to develop anxiety or depression. Some women develop a panic disorder during menopause. You're blessed if your friends and family members provide you with valuable social support. However, it may happen, that you may be all alone by yourself, none to talk with and share your concern or plight. sometimes it helps to connect with other women in your community who may be going through perimenopause or menopause. Remember, you're not alone, there are others who are also going through such changes. Here comes the crucial point to exhibit courage and determination to fight your demons.

Steps to manage hormones and mental health

Being strongly positive and stay optimistic

Avoid any task or person creating conflict (big destroyer of peace of mind)

Avoid negativity & pessimism at any cost (big source inviting self-destruction)

Getting regular physical exercise

Having a balanced diet & enough sleep every day

Minimizing stress in daily routine

Visit your doctor to rule out any physical reasons for your symptoms like thyroid problems

Lifestyle changes, medications, therapy, multivitamins or a combination of these options

Avoid smoking, caffeine and harmful habits

Try Relaxation Techniques like Yoga, meditation, and massage-they help reduce stress and induce better sleep at night

Seek Support Groups and make new friends, share your concerns and joy with others

Academic stress, anxiety & depression

Anxiety and depression are currently the most common mental health diagnoses among school and college students world over. Academic stress is a mental distress associated with some estimated frustration related to academic failure. It can occur to any school or college going student irrespective of age, gender or academic performance. Anxiety and depression are associated with high levels of worry and tension that can affect academic performance of students. At times even perception of the probability of failure also leads to fear and anxiety.

Researchers have investigated the connection between anxiety, academic performance, and working memory and have found that as students' levels of anxiety, depression, and worry increased, academic performance decreased. Positive stress or eustress (also called good stress) can lead you to accomplish your goals and allow you to be successful. In this kind of stress, you may consider a stressful condition as an opportunity that may produce good outcome for you.

Globally, exam anxiety is a prevalent phenomenon. Exam fear or Test anxiety is a combination of physiological and psychological over-stimulation and stress with worry, dread, fear of failure that occur before or during exams. Adolescents experience considerable stress these days in multiple areas irrespective of their academic ability and performance due to various reasons such as constant worry about examinations, pear pressure, unfair tests, too much work in some subjects, fear of failure, parental expectations, wanting to be more popular or fear about future. Poor study habits, no or bad preparation, poor past test performance, social challenges and an underlying apprehension problem can all contribute to exam/test anxiety. Hence, assessment and management of stress among adolescents must be given priority.

In a competitive world, students too often feel themselves incompetent and useless when they're unable to achieve what they want to due to any reason. Frequently, they have aim to be like some achiever who looks and perform very smart, intelligent and is successful. They try hard to be like the one, but unable to achieve that level and this failure leads to frustration. Hence, they take undesirable, shocking steps to harm themselves. There are plenty of reasons and conditions for that. Every so often, we come across the tragic news of students committing suicide by jumping off the top of a parking garage, strangling or suffocating themselves, hanging from a tree or ceiling fan, drowning in river or sea, consuming poison or stabbing self. They are so frustrated and depressed that they can never see any hope in life for themselves.

Academic Stress management

Both parents and teachers can play an important role in minimizing or eradicating academic stress for students. Since children and teens spend most of the day in classrooms, teachers are the best individuals to play a powerful role in helping them. Also friends, families, relatives and every one of us too can contribute by helping our students in various ways-by understanding them, by friendly counseling, rightful guidance, suggestions, encouragement and motivational strategies. We as a conscious and thoughtful community must help each other to live a happy, peaceful and content life. It's our prime responsibility and obligation towards society too.

Parents can help-

It is obvious that when children suffer from stress, it affects the whole family. Normally, the parents are believed to be trouble shooters for the children and can fix their problems. Hence, when they feel clueless and don't know how to help the children in their academic stress, it can be frustrating for them. This may even add to stress in the home. However, parents can act by realizing and adopting strategies to reduce symptoms of toxic stress as follows-

Every child is unique academically and intellectually, so method of learning differs

Reduce stress by scheduling study, sports and other activities around what works best for individual child

Serve a healthy, nutritional diet

Ensure the right amount of sleep

Incorporate daily physical exercise routine (great distractor from study-stress)

Teach children self-care strategies

Teachers can help-

Teachers can work together with students as a team to avoid and reducing stress

By talking about issues bothering students

By involving students in academic and extracurricular activities to make them feel more in control

By limiting homework/class work overload

By providing academic support whenever student need it

By being available to provide emotional support and motivation whenever needed

Job depression:

Researchers say that being in a job that you hate is worse for your mental health than being unemployed. When a person's mental health is affected by anxiety and depression, it often manifests in physical problems as well. Those who are depressed or suffer from anxiety often eat too less or too much, leading to obesity, diabetes and cardiac problems. Lack of good leadership is prevailing in many workplaces these days. Many fall victims to anxiety and depression due to work pressures, peer pressure and performance pressure. So many suffer under dismal and often weak leadership. They either leave for another job or suffer in silence. I was probably the best example in this case, who preferred to leave instead of suffering in silence.

Job/workplace traps can lead to depression and anxiety. Some of them include: Job insecurity due to fear of getting fired or laid off any time, irregular work hours and weak leadership, Too bossy work culture, No consistent schedule with lack of enough rest to recharge, Struggling to maintain family relationships and feeling burdened owing to work-life interference, Feeling like you have no control, No say in decision-making, No one to talk to about your issues at work, Workplace discrimination or harassment, Hostile/ nonharmonies work environments, No match-your values with work culture—All of these bring lots of job dissatisfaction and anxiety leading to higher risks of depression and further anxiety.

What can you do for yourself in this situation? You may best take appropriate steps as follows:

Detect your status- whether you're stressed, or depressed, and the reason behind it.

How much you can take it, if you're stressed out.

Do the job you love or try to love the job you do.

Take steps to regain control so that you don't feel overwhelmed.

Take breaks and start again to check if you feel better.

Leave the job if it is killing you gradually and you can't take it anymore.

Speak your mind, if you're right, keeping in mind not to hurt some-

one unreasonably.

Never take decision in hurry. But, if you ain't happy, wait, finally decide and LEAVE!

Go find the work you can enjoy with better productivity and appreciation.

People talk a lot about never burning your bridges when you are in a situation of whether to stay or leave the job. Since you're the one who has to live with your reality, if you're sure that you're never going to cross it again anyway, then I would say go ahead and set on fire those bridges which are actually burning you every day and acting as hindrance to your growth.

In my opinion, if you don't look forward to going to your work every morning and instead get headache, that place is not for you! Change your job, sooner is better for you-for your physical, mental, and emotional health, and personal and professional growth as well.

Best case-You do what you love. Ok Case-You love what you do. Worst case-You hate what you do. Leave it if you can't Love, and you would Love that Leaving.

Timing, stress, worry and anxiety:

Everyone has their own timing and strength. Don't be troubled by the length of time it took you to chart your own course. You may be slow than others. Don't compare your progress, your life and life events with those of others and feel stressed out. Feeling timed out, left out and jealousy lead to nowhere in life but leave you with lots of depression and anxiety. Too much worry, stress and anxiety may lead to criminal activities and suicidal ideations. Don't worry excessively for your future too. We all must arrive at the destination in life on our own schedule. Take only the trip when you're ready, and the timing won't be more perfect.

Stress is a reactive phenomenon to a threat in a situation. Anxiety is a consequence to the stress. Stress does interfere with most people's lives at mild to moderate level, in good or bad times. During the period of stress, nervous system reacts by releasing a flood of stress hormones, including adrenaline and cortisol, which rouse the body for emergency action. The heart pounds faster, muscles tighten, blood pressure rises, breath quickens, and the senses become sharper. Most people cope up with such low-level stress reasonably well. Chronic stress, nonetheless, can affect your health, causing symptoms from headaches, fatigue, loss of appetite or overeating, irritation, high BP, and chest pain to heart palpitations, skin rashes, and loss of sleep.

Different people react differently to chronic stress. They may exhibit any or many of behavioral, psychological, physical, cognitive or social changes. Basically, these changes can be categorized as- defensive, protective, attacking, destructive or combating reactions to stress. Confident and positive minded people react to stress by keeping their stress in perspective and assuming a good solution exists. They take timely decision, right number of responsibilities, keep expectations fair and reasonable and ask for help if needed. Weak, vulnerable and negative people react to stress by feeling overwhelmed, unmotivated, emotionally exhausted and bad decisions. In severe conditions, they may succumb to overwhelming stress by killing self or others.

Suicidal thoughts and tendency are common among those who can't handle stress anymore and undergo severe depression. Most people who experience suicidal ideation don't carry it through, although some may make suicide attempts. Suicide is one of the most common causes of death among students due to academic stress. Anyone who has suicidal thoughts should ask for help.

Believe in yourself. Be mentally strong and confident. Anxiety and depression do commonly attack the emotionally and morally weaker section of people. So, be bold and raise above the adversities. Consider the adversity in your life as passing phase of life. Tough time doesn't last forever, but the tough individual will! Please remember—Nothing can strengthen the judgement and harden the individual better than adversities of human life. You're powerful and your voice will be prevailing. Learn the value of your own timing as well as your inner strength. Identify your inner power and you can rule the roost.

Decision fatigue:

During the period of my anxiety and depression, I experienced terrible decision fatigue, which I took long to realize. Decision fatigue is a term used for that feeling when you're overly stressed by the vast number of decisions you've to take throughout the day. Our brains can suffer from mental fatigue just as our bodies can become physically fatigued after a long workout. The feeling was different from mundane physical fatigue. I wasn't consciously aware of being tired, but was low on mental energy, per se. Throughout the day, I was juggling many demands of my life. I had tight hourly schedules at work and often juggled several tasks at once at home. No matter how sensible and principled you try to be, you can't make decision after decision without paying a biological price—I realized after paying price through my terrible condition.

Every decision we make uses up our psychological and emotional energies. No matter how strong you're, your ability to make the best decisions can eventually fail due to decision fatigue. Just a simple act of thinking about a trivial matter tires one out and reduces one's brainpower. It's a psychological condition. It reduces your decision-making ability. The more decisions you make throughout the day, brain starts losing its ability to comprehend, processing information and cognition. In extreme situations, it may lead to structural degeneration and impaired functioning of the hippocampus (part of the brain which regulates motivation, emotion and memory). This may lead to an increased risk of developing neuropsychiatric disorders, including depression, dementia or nervous breakdown.

Ducking a decision often creates bigger problems in long run. It lessens the mental strain momentarily, however. Unfortunately, people don't have much insight into this problem condition. They lack knowledge about mental fatigue and its resulting decision fatigue — even while making decisions that can be life-changing for such individuals. Decision fatigue helps us understand why normally sensible individuals get enraged at friends, families or colleagues needlessly and do nasty behavior at times or can't resist easily avoidable temptations that may be harmful to them.

If you're constantly worrying every day about little decisions like what to wear at work, what to cook or eat, what music to listen or movie to watch, you'll become more mentally exhausted as the day progresses. Hence, try to make the life simpler and easier. Life isn't as complex as we make it by messing with it, I realized with my experience. Avoid making a simple thing intricate. Preserve your mental power for important decisions of the day. Don't waste your intellect and skills by pondering too much on inconsequential or insignificant matters of life. Live the life as it comes to you. Live each day, every moment, fully. Take baby steps and enjoy your achievements of every day. Learn to mechanize everyday decisions so that you don't have to constantly think about them and waste your brainpower. I learnt my life lessons through my conditions and realized that however big your problem may be, life is certainly bigger than that. Respect Life instead of giving too much importance to problems.

Decision making is a process of making choices by identifying a decision, collecting information, and gauging alternative solutions. By a step-by-step decision-making process, we can organize relevant information, define alternatives effectively and avoid decision fatigue.

Simple practices to surmount decision fatigue and boost willpower can be:

Simplify, streamline, make things easier.

Prioritize your work and activities—Do the most important thing first.

Plan your routine decisions well in advance.

Choose the simpler or easier option instead of long, complex one.

Limit your options to avoid distraction and complexity.

Reduce the number of decisions you make throughout the day.

Good enough is good enough. You can't be perfectionist all the time, admit it and attempt.

Stop making important decisions in haste.

Don't forget to declutter your life

Decluttering of your life is as much essential as getting rid of things you do not need or want from your home or office. We must throw out all negative emotions, thoughts and NEGATIVITY from our minds and life. The way clutter attracts dust, dirt, and even mold, in life these negative vibes and emotions impact the quality of our lives and ruin our inner peace and happiness. Decluttering is an important way to practice self-care since it helps to take control of our life to improve our overall physical and mental well-being, making us more confident and successful.

Physical exercise and Yoga

Exercise is another way that you may use to assist your mood. Exercise and yoga produce endorphins and other happy hormones in the brain that act as natural painkillers—and also improve the ability to sleep and self-image, which in turn reduce stress. This may be a method of release for you.

Activities like walking or jogging involving repetitive muscle movements are stress relieving too. Even few minutes of aerobic exercise can stimulate anti-anxiety effects. It has been observed that at least 30 minutes of exercise a day for 3-5 days/week may significantly improve depression or anxiety symptoms. Like any other cardiovascular exercise, brisk walking boosts endorphins, which can reduce stress hormones and alleviate mild depression.

Yoga is a mind-body practice that combines physical poses, controlled breathing, and meditation or relaxation. The pleasures and benefits of yoga are widely understood. Yoga, as an excellent stress-relief exercise, involves a series of moving and stationary postures combined with deep breathing. It may help reduce stress, lower blood pressure and lower your heart rate as well. Yoga can strengthen body's natural relaxation response and bring into a healthy balance. It can improve muscle strength, flexibility, blood circulation, oxygen uptake and hormone function.

Self-soothing techniques of yoga can prevent onset of anxiety and enhance mental focus. It also reduces anxiety, modulating the stress response system. Few studies have shown that yoga can help improve sleep pattern in chronic insomnia and stress. Some of the various yoga poses such as Legs-Up-The-Wall Pose (Viparita Karani) and Restorative Bridge Pose (Setu Bandha Sarvangasana) help to bend and stretch body to a great night's rest.

Sleep and Sex:

A good night's sleep is, of course, one of the most important requirements of keeping yourself healthy, accomplished, cognitively sharp, physically strong, and in a good mood for whole day. Sex facilitates bonding and feelings of intimacy with your partner, makes you feel warm and fuzzy and actually reduces anxiety and boosts your overall health.

Continuous lack of sleep or poor sleep and sex quality make you feel tired, groggy and irritable the next day. It can drastically affect overall health, making you prone to medical conditions such as obesity, diabetes, heart disease, high BP and may even lead to an increased risk of Alzheimer's disease. It can lead to trouble concentrating at work, feeling sluggish and indulging in outlandish behavior against a normal nature. Continuous nights of bad sleep and bad sex can put a serious damper on your every next day routine. As such, there are more than a few nascent culprits that can be to blame for sleepless nights. Studies suggest that sexual activity may be linked with- good mental health, increased levels of trust, intimacy, and love in the relationships. Like physical exercise, a pleasing sex can help reduce stress and anxiety and increase happiness.

When you're really worried about something while going to the bed, it's much harder for you to fall into sleep and your body to relax itself into a sound slumber. Emotions and stress of any kind can definitely play a vital role in quality of sleep and sexual activities. Pleasant feelings and contentment through good sex help inducing blissful sleep, on the other hand, negative feelings, tension and anxiety during sex may ruin the pleasure of a sound sleep. Being under stress can actually lead to something called *hyperarousal* which, according to the National Sleep Foundation, can upset balance between sleep and wakefulness. Consequently, it is of great value figuring out what can make the sleep restful, invigorating and enjoyable. Same is true for sex. It may be very easy said than done, nonetheless, one can improve upon sleep and sex pattern by determination, changing attitude towards life and happenings, and rest assured, where there's a will, there's a way — to get to a better-quality sleep and sex.

Some of the proven methods I would like to recommend at this juncture, which actually helped me when I was in the deep state of anxiety and depression and sleep was an elusive phenomenon.

I practiced good sleep hygiene checklist. I still practice the healthy sleep practice which I started during the period of my crisis, which still helps me a great deal. My regimen included— a consistent bedtime routine, knowing about how much sleep I need, going to bed same time every night, finding a quiet place to sleep, keeping my bedroom cozy, using bed only for sleep and relaxation and no other work-related things, limiting TV and mobile time before going to bed and also avoiding any daytime naps. I focused on my sex life. My regular, pleasing sex life benefited me a great deal in my recovery, I can say so. Since all these healthy sleep and sex habits helped me make a big difference in my quality of life, I'd like to recommend the same to others who are struggling with insomnia or bad quality sleep. Hope they may help them as well.

Try to cultivate a bedtime routine that's all about self-care, relaxing and comforting. Chatting with a close friend or watching a comedy or pleasant TV show or movie before sleeping can be very helpful. You may switch off your mobiles and TV screens about an hour before bed and sex, and instead turn on some calming, soothing instrumental music and meditate for some time. Listening to a soothing music of my choice and a guided meditation helped me a lot. Taking a shower before going to sleep (hot water during winter and cold water in summer) refreshes body and mind and assists in restful sleep and invigorating sex at night. Adding into your night regimen some essential oil or aroma therapy before sleep help clear your mind so you can slowly fall into a state of total and utter relaxation.

Make it a rule: Your bedroom is for sleeping not for any work-related activities. This is generally found true with very busy, workaholic individuals, who carry their work to their beds and unable to find time to relax due to incessant anxiety concerning workload. Often times, our thoughts are dominated by regrets or mistakes of the past, or anxiety about impending events. We're unable to perform what needs to be done at the moment because we're trapped in either past or future. If you want to avoid worry, don't fret about the future. Just live each day until bedtime. Simple living is the key to a happy life. You must follow one of Dale Carnegie's principles for overcoming worry as to live in "day-tight compartments."

If you're overwhelmed with worries and simply cannot concentrate because of anxiety, straight away confront yourself. Talk to yourself and sort the matter out before it's too late. Ask yourself few questions such as—What is the problem? What is the cause of the problem? How it can be resolved? What is the worst that can possibly happen due to the problem? Now, comes the strategies—Acknowledge the problem, prepare to accept the worst. Try to solve the problem but, don't ponder upon the problem deliberately and remind yourself of the exorbitant price you can pay for worry in terms of your physical and mental health.

Wisdom says to remember—Avoid any sort of displeasing encounter, negative thoughts and unpleasant activity, especially before going to bed. This is must to avail a blissful sleep. I was used to chant prayers and concentrate on divine bliss before going to bed, which helped me a lot to win over my woes.

I believed that the prayer is the raising of the mind and heart to God or the requesting of good things from God. I observed that practice reduced my nightmarish and waking up in the middle of nights. Even making sure you do physical exercise every day to get out some of those extra agitations going on in your mind will help.

Body Energies and Mental Health

During my mental illness, I was overwhelmed, stressed out and anxious day after day. I wanted to do anything and everything to get back to myself like I used to be before. I wanted to re-write whole new chapter of my life with self-help. At one point of time, it seemed to me that really nothing will work consistently until I discovered the power of energy within. I realized and admitted the tremendous negative effects of the negativity and positive effects of optimism. When I became determined to do absolute makeover of myself, that's when everything changed.

I was reading about body and body energies, and their incredible effects on our physical and mental health and wellbeing. I learnt human body's existence in various significant parts affecting individual's health. As per some psychological theory, human bodies are made up of 4 distinct parts—physical, emotional, mental, and spiritual, and each body should be balanced to have a healthy life, physical and mental wellness, and understanding our existence. All 4 parts play central role in making us feel strong, confident and healthy-physically, mentally, emotionally and spiritually. With all parts balanced, we feel a connection with a higher force/energy/divine existence.

I also learnt that within our body, we've many major and minor energy centres called Chakras, which typically are 7 to 8 in number and connected to major organs and glands of the body. These chakras are responsible for affecting the life energy, which is also known as Qi or Praana. Each chakra impacts our mental health in different ways-through mood, psychologically and physically. The Heart Charka is the Centre of the Chakra System and processes our energy into feelings. When these Chakras become imbalanced or blocked, may be due to negative energies, they affect our mental health and stability. They may also lead to disease or mental illness, panic/anxiety, depression, stress, anger, and other physical problems. A stressful environment, life problems, losses, or traumatic events can create blockages in energy flow that can translate into mental symptoms like anxiety and depression. Balancing chakras help restore our energy flow and alleviate anxiety. Many Asian healing traditions Chinese medicine, Ayurveda, and Tibetan medicine use a combination of physical, psychological, and spiritual approaches to treat energetic imbalances and restore optimal mental and physical health.

I understood the concept of body energies and how they can affect us positively and negatively. There is a definite science behind how we act, interact or feel with the people having positive or negative vibes. Once I acknowledged the actuality that energy within me-both negative and positive energies- were affecting my reality and my health, I started plunging into exploration and mastering my body kinetics/energies. Soon after, the healing process of my energetic body and mind began and the life started happening 'for me', instead of 'to me'. As I went on acquiring knowledge about my body energies, I became a healer for myself.

I saw many changes subsequent to this phenomenal transformation in myself. I started becoming more confident and vibrant. I was at peace with myself. There was more liveliness, vitality and enthusiasm inside me. I started feeling like ME-Original ME- again. The things I ever wanted most in my life started coming to me, naturally and consistently. There were good people- optimistic and lively people in my life; I could nurture better and healthier associations into my life, with negative relations started fading away. I stayed away from the negative-minded people and talks. I started training my mind to see positivity in most negative situation. I constantly said to myself *"there is always some positivity in every negative situation"* and surprisingly, I found that proving to be true every now and then! It was- my positive energy and optimistic mindset- which were making me happy and successful in most of the situations now, I realized.

Finally, I was free of my negativity, anxiety and evil senses inhabiting in my mind for long time. Happiness and joy of life were not any more a "dream" but a reality for me!

Love yourself

Love yourself and don't hate—an important moral advise for an individual suffering from mental health. You may develop self-hatred and start blaming yourself for your failure, your miserable condition, the wrong choice you made or putting you in the trouble or stressful condition.

The phenomenon of self-hate has been observed in many cases when people with mental health issue are unable to cope up with their problems. They feel totally helpless and miserable. They develop feelings of self-rejection and self-neglect and may start thinking to harm themselves-by injuring or committing suicide. It was true for me that I was absolutely dejected and down with my anxiety, overpowering stress and depression. I was feeling myself unfortunate to have to go through all those stressful days and months. I was in fact, repentant about the reality that I was wasting my precious time by doing nothing productive during that time of my suffering. There were terrible feelings of—guilt, shame, hatred, regret, boredom and exhaustion, just to name a few. It was such an overwhelming feeling, unable to describe in any words.

I'd a great problem with my nostalgic memories, which was quite weird! I deliberately avoided watching good, old, classical movies from 60's, 70's or 80's era and old TV programs; avoided listening to old classical music from the same era, contrary to the fact that I always remained fond of nostalgia. Nostalgia always brought me feelings of happiness, increased my joyful mood and heighted positive emotions, which resulted as the feelings of warmth and affection from nostalgic reflections. Nonetheless, at this time, nostalgic memories were compelling me to react into grief, apathy, hopelessness and indifference.

I had problem with my hormones too. I was in perimenopausal phase. I was experiencing stress, mood swings, either high or low mood, and anxiety. At times, I would have hot flashes, crying spells and felt irritable. I got distressing thoughts and felt a range of emotions. I was terrified by the very thoughts of getting old, ugly and disliked by everyone! Every day, I looked in the mirror to see a face that I could recognize as my own and to check for any sudden unwelcome facial changes. Sometimes, I would stare at my eyes and face in mirror for a long time. After a while of staring, I could see my face all warped and creepy-it was scary! I felt as if my brain was trying to scare me.

It was hard for me to love myself at that juncture. My fear, anxiety and self-doubt were strong enough to diminish the values of my attributes and abilities in my own eyes. It was a sort of fierce sense of oppression, the first symptom of which was losing my ability to dream. Then my power to positive thinking was gone. My determination faded with doubt. Confidence and hope were simply given away. Joy and Happiness were far away. The state of my mind was in total disarray and decay. My negative thought process was adding further woes by making me believe that there was no hope for me to recover from the ill fate of mine.

Eventually, while being on the path of self-discovery and recovery, I realized my own shortcomings-my internal fears and negative thought processes and started working upon them to do what worked best for me. I agree that life is never smooth for all people all the time. Ups and downs are inevitable elements of any balanced life. Hence, it's vital to understand that if you can't change the circumstances, you must change your attitude, change yourself.

Look at the brighter side of the situation, I told myself. When I realized my problem and developed strong desire to overcome it, I started working upon the solution. Initially, I received strong resistance from within, I became successful eventually, nevertheless. I became more oriented and more focused to be a healthy person- physically and mentally after my resolve. I reverted back to my healthy food habits, sleep pattern and lifestyle. My drive to achieve healthy weight and stay there, eat healthy diet with enough calcium, vitamins and minerals helped me resolve my health issues with my eyes, hair, nails, teeth and other body parts which I was facing since my anxiety and depression days. I increased my walking exercise and enhanced positive—thinking and reading habits. Everything would be just great, every day I encouraged myself.

From my own example and strategies that I adopted for myself and which worked best for me, I would like to share here with all silent sufferers with the hope that they get benefited.

I'd emphasize- in any given situation, know your value. Human life is very precious, value it. No matter what people do or say, and regardless of what happens to you, you alone can control how you feel about yourself. Remind yourself that you're priceless, you're unique. You may be having many flaws, but you definitely possess many extraordinary, positive qualities, which you should elaborate to regain your lost confidence and strength. Be aware of your strength and virtues. Unleash that abundant source of power hidden inside. Show yourself that you're strong enough to be on your own. Dig into the reason of your plight and analyze the situation, instead of being judgmental and sentimental about the problem. Best help is self-help, trust this. If its hormones that are troubling you, wait for the time to get them settle down. Be patient. Don't lose your perseverance, composure and peace of mind while comparing others' achievements with your failures. Instead, love yourself for what you're and keep striving to be better each day than previous day.

Remember-your struggle is with yourself and not others; your competitor is You, yourself, not others. Rise above adversities and shine bright. Misfortune won't last long, but 'confident You' will, for sure. Set your priorities; start working upon them with firm vigor, grit and tenacity. Don't ever stop learning and growing as a person. Change your thinking, change your life. Strength, struggle, resolve, hope, desires, dream, happiness, love, respect, pride-all are vital elements of your life. Just be yourself. Love yourself. Love your abilities and thresholds. Believe me, they're and always will serve as your foundation for happy and content life.

One of my personal mottos is "stay happy and keep smiling". I believe that happiness is tied to making healthy choices with my life in everything I do- eating food, people I stay in company with, the way I talk to others and myself. Nevertheless, it became challenging to make that choice in recent years as I endured many losses such as the death of my father and my beloved dog, unfortunate developments such as leaving my medical practice, my patients and my students with whom I shared strong bonding, my home, and my longtime friends.

During the period of my anxiety and depression, with the resolve to help myself, I went through various informative literature, books and write ups on diverse mental health issues. It was initially pretty much unpleasant to do self-psychiatric counselling. It was really embarrassing to find myself reading books on rational behavior in adverse conditions, self-motivation and self-reassurance instead of motivating and educating others on the same issues. It was like a learned teacher had been an ignorant student, and now she was requiring guidance in order to acquire awareness about the same thing which she was preaching others for years! The table had turned. Anyway, I'd accepted the fact and had moved on.

During the same time, I chanced upon some very useful guides and literature, the knowledge and information on the crucial topic of mental health which I honestly tried to apply in my endeavor to my recovery. In one of the editions of the Diagnostic and Statistical Manual of Mental Disorders, several different types of anxiety disorders are listed. I agreed that I had symptoms of, undeniably, few of them.

I was having panic attacks—sudden, intense periods of extraordinary terror, rapid breathing, sweating and chest pain—several times a day.

I was apprehensive-most part of the day, living with the nervousness and anticipation of imminent disasters- can be diagnosed as: generalized anxiety disorder.

I'd developed different kinds of phobias as well such as: flying, driving on highways, taking medications, can be diagnosed as: specific and general phobia.

I'd developed unease in dealing and communicating with people. I was avoiding meeting people. It was not reflecting in my apparent behavior, though-can be diagnosed as: social phobia.

I'd developed many no-go zones such as long queues, movie, shopping malls since I feared potential for panic attacks anywhere, anytime—can be diagnosed as: agoraphobia.

Various strong negative feelings like-loss of inner happiness, uselessness, incompetence being rejected, snubbed, or ignored by others—all happen when you have no happy event in life to look forward to. Life turns lusterless, dull and sad. There is no feeling of excitement and joy. Every moment seems like a burden. Life appears like a liability. You live-just because you can't die, not because you're enjoying life. Life seems like a punishment, but for what, you don't know. You just keep suffering—every moment, every day and every night. It's really a horrible feeling. It's like you've been trapped. There's no way to escape from the trap. Only death can rescue you.

While going through the hell of my plight, I read something very meaningful, deep and insightful—that "when God wants to move you to higher ground, he may remove the soft feathers of your comfort zone so that you can experience the painful thorns. The purpose is not to harm you, but to inform you that it's time to fly to higher ground. Be encouraged when you're facing difficulties in life, He who is Mighty may be doing mighty things for His purposes to be fulfilled". This divine knowledge provided tremendous peace to my troubled mind, restored my lost love and faith to myself. It did provide with eternal peace, patience and perseverance to my aggrieved psychological and physical existence.

Life has ever been a trial and error. One who tries, may fail few times but in the end that failure is worthy enough to learn important life lessons and succeed. Life is full of trials and tribulations. We must endure our trials and learn the best lessons so that, whenever required, we can look in the eyes of another sufferer with absolute empathy, sympathy, profound understanding, and perfect credibility and can say, " I've empathy for you. I've been through the same struggle. I know your pain. You can do this; look, I've been there and have prevailed over it."

Depression can hit anyone, irrespective of their financial/ social status. Even wealthy, successful and celebrities with enviable lives can suffer. According to the World Economic Forum, depression is now a disorder affecting above 250 million people globally. According to CMHA (Canadian Mental Health Association) Mental illness affects all Canadians at some time through a family member, friend or colleague. Mental illness affects people of all ages, cultures or income levels. In any given year, 1 in 5 people in Canada may personally experience a mental health issue. Nearly 8% of adults experience major depression at some time in their lives.

Everyone feels depressed every so often, however clinical depression is a serious ailment that entails feeling low or empty continuously, exhaustion, loss of interest in activities, insomnia, loss of appetite, etc. It wreaks havoc on your personal life and physical health, and, in extreme cases, can lead to murder or suicide. Simply because someone appears to be very happy, cheerful or successful outside doesn't mean that's how are inside. Some people acquire art of faking and can easily wear their masks to hide their inner sorrow and pain. It did happen in my case. I kept suffering for a pretty long time-for few years precisely, nevertheless, people close to me, even my colleagues and friends never came to know what was going on inside me. My loneliness, my depression was killing me inside, but outside I was disguising a usual, fearless person. This could have proven destructive too, though.

Studies published in Clinical Psychological Science have revealed certain ways in which you can potentially spot depression in your loved ones by paying attention to the types of words they use. Spotting depression in a friend or loved one isn't always as easy as you might think, though. Researchers have found that people suffering from depression often tend to use words like "nothing," "never," "everyone," and "everything." They also observed them using a lot of negative adjectives and adverbs, such as "lonely," "sad," or "miserable". Moreover, people with anxiety and depression are inclined to use substantially more first-person singular pronouns, like "I," "me," and "myself," which may signify how lonely and isolated they feel in the world. This pattern can suggest people with stress and depression are more focused on themselves, and less connected with others. I was feeling the same during my period of depression and anxiety.

I've learnt my life lessons through my anxiety and depression conditions. I've stopped negative self-talk to reduce stress. I've got better understanding of anxiety, depression, stress, and all other mental health issues now. I hate negativity of any sort much more than ever before. I stay away from negative minded people and depressive environment. I enjoy basking in the glow of nostalgia. The pleasant reminiscence of things gone by provides me an instant reprieve from the pressures of mundane, hectic and future-oriented world. I recognize my subconscious power which helped me discover a positive self-concept. I've started caring for myself and learnt to love and parent myself. I value happiness, compassion and success in life better than before. I love my life and want to make the best of it. I tend to feel happier, loved and valued. I also have higher self-esteem, feel closer to myself and feel that life has more meaning.

My heart and mind have increased perceptions of social support and I'm more willing to help the people when people are lonely. I do feel things I never felt before. I meet people with a different point of view. I try to live a life that I could be proud of. I have the courage to start all over again. I simply think about making my life better and meaningful – with whatever highs and lows may come on the way. My attitude towards the people have changed, especially, those appear to be anxious or stressed out due to any sort of stress in their daily living. My love and compassion for animals, old people and mentally ill individuals have grown many folds.

Today I am very sympathetic and compassionate than ever before to all those suffering from mental health issues. I've turned softer, caring, empathetic and considerate to all those who need my help in any way. I feel privileged and humble to help others in their deeds and needs. I like to remind the sufferers of mental health that they are not alone. Writing of this book is also my way of rendering a contribution to encourage, motivate and inspire others who are going through similar conditions to come forward, prevail over their problems, get back to their original lively self and live happy life, becoming role models for others.

I realize the significance of happiness in life. I've appreciated the fact that happiness is a highest form of health-physical, mental and emotional. Half of the health issues are related with your happiness and contentment in life. Being happy improves the quality of your life. According to recent studies, it also increases the quantity of your life too. Older people were found to be drastically less likely to die early and may live a bit longer if they remain happy, excited, and content on everyday basis. My parents and grandparents are the classic example of this phenomena. I found my father, who died at the age of 87, always happy and content with his life until his death due to natural cause. My mother too, who is nearly 90, always remain cheerful and joyous expressing her gratitude for a happy, healthy life.

Your happiness is the reflection of your health. Happiness is really nothing more than good health and a bad memory. Our greatest happiness doesn't rely upon the condition of life in which our destiny has placed us but is always the outcome of a good mental and physical health, good conscience, work, and freedom in all activities. For every minute you're stressed out, you may lose 60 seconds of happiness, we must understand. "Happiness isn't a when or a where; it can be a here and a now. But until you're happy with who you're you will never be happy because of what you have." I found this very applicable in every situation.

I've started living in the present to enjoy and feel the life. I do have expectations from my future; however, life will take its own course, I understand, and just hope for the best ever. I keep myself away from being unduly anxious and restless over future prospects. Today is a good day and the *'Best is coming'* I keep motivating myself. I trust—everything will be fine. I work very hard each day and rely upon my destiny to reward me suitably. I agree that not all hardworking people may be successful always and not all successful people may be hardworking either. However, that philosophy is never a deterrent for me to work hard since success is subjectively defined and subjective success is an individual's response to an objective situation, I perceive.

◆ ◆ ◆

My advice to those who are undergoing the rage of anxiety or depression in their lives is very simple and straightforward—

Don't strive hard to prove yourself when you're not in positive frame of mind. If the day ahead weighs heavy and your works feel like tortures, there's no need to hesitate in reorganizing your routine. If the morning brings you sadness and gloom, its ok to stay in bed. I changed my routine to help myself when I felt an urge to sleep more and didn't feel like doing anything under the morning blues.

Its ok if you don't feel like taking shower sometimes or washing your hair for few days. Don't make yourself feel worse if you fear water while showering or bath feels like you'll be drawn. I'd developed a terrible fear of water (hydrophobia), especially while showering. Even approaching or being near water would trigger my brain responses. Water intimidated me, I realized. So, I avoided taking shower whenever possible. I didn't feel guilty for not being clean and neat. Being happy is more important than being hygienic, I perceived! Peace within, serenity and being self-confident are more important than being perfectionist and precise here.

Remember-a day is not a lifetime. Resting is not a rusting always. Relaxing a while does not lead to your defeat. In this competitive world, moving at a faster pace is desirable, nonetheless, when you're exhausted, reducing your speed and taking a breather are best ideas. Laying low when tide is high is a wise decision and it won't be considered your failure. Its ok to take a break from an anxious, shattered and unorganized mind, the world won't come to an end, for sure! The mountain will still be there when you want to try again, you may climb them at your own pace and time, once you feel better and be ready.

JUST LOVE YOURSELF WHILE WAITING FOR RIGHT TIME. CONFIDENCE WILL FOLLOW AUTOMATICALY.

"Life may be tough at few points, but Destiny is not created by the Shoes we wear but by the Steps we take, you're the creator of your Destiny." This has become a motivating sentence for me. I just remember one thing—Karma. 'Try to do your best and leave on Almighty the rest' I follow the simple belief in my life.

All of us have Challenges in life to face, our own demons to deal with, may be on everyday basis. Life is not fair and easy on anyone. Life's unfairness doesn't give you license to walk wrong path, though. In adversities, weak minded people opt for one of the two proclivities- kill self(suicide) or kill other(murder). No matter how much injustice we may get, how many times we were humiliated or fell down from grace, what matters is how you react at that very point of time and next. Your Mind (conscience) exactly knows what Right (Dharma) is. Negativity of mind will kill you and others. Positivity is vibrant and contagious, and we need it.

What is your life worth? A happy life or a tragic unnatural end?! How much lonely you are only you know! In the struggle of survival in the busy life, every day we are losing beautiful people from our planet. Loneliness hurts but letting someone suffer silently will hurt more. Please try to give love, care, attention, and warmth to those sufferers and make earth a better place!

Today, I acknowledge that however big your problem may be, life is certainly bigger than that. Respect human life, it is our precious gift from our creator. The most exotic happening of life is—possibility to lead a simple living. It's an extraordinary privilege to have an ordinary life! Respect Life more than giving too much significance to your problems. Problems exist just because life exists. No life, no problems. Life always prevails, in every situation-good or bad, conducive or unfavorable. Life never gets defeated, problems do. Life is the real Hero in the end of our story of our existence, not our problems—with this enlightenment I conclude my story. I want to shine my light of enlightenment every day and want to touch the life of sufferers to transform it the way it did happen to me. Depression and anxiety need not only professional care, but very personal too! Be the giver!

The story of Dr. Liza draws to a close here, but the journey in the search of meaningfulness in life continues. Life will always be back to its scheming ways, however, there will be more hopes and success in the future, so, Stay Tuned.........

AFTERWORD

Hi Readers! I hope that this story has gotten your attention and you enjoyed the contents of this book.

Thank you all for going through this book. Your comments about your reading experience of this book is valuable for me. If you have any comments, please email me (**bookauthor@ live.com**).

I would appreciate your comments.

Stay happy and blessed!

.

ACKNOWLEDGEMENT

This is a motivational and inspiring story of one of my acquaintances- Dr. Liza Fernandez (Name has been changed for confidentiality), a Psychiatry professor herself, and sufferer of the comorbidity of Anxiety and Depression, someone who fought successfully her severe mental health issue of anxiety, depression, stress, social anxiety, and finally emerging victorious through her determination and resolve. Names of the places and people in the story have been changed along with necessary alterations in the story with kind permission of Dr. Liza to maintain privacy and confidentiality. There is no intention to hurt anyone's sentiments. Motivation and inspiration remain the sole purpose of publishing this story and this book.

The story in the book has been written in the narrator's own words to keep its purity and appeal.

I take this opportunity to thank Dr. Liza Fernandez for sharing her story with me, allowing me to interview her, publish and share her real-life story to the world through this book.

ABOUT THE AUTHOR

Prof. (Dr) Usha Dabas

Prof (Dr.) Usha Dabas is a Healthcare Professional, Educationist and Author with over 30 years of academic, clinical and administrative expertise in the fields of Medicine, Dentistry and Healthcare. She has authored nearly 10 Textbooks on the general and specialty subject matters of Medical and Dental Health Science. She is Director, Healthcare Faculty at Springfield College of Healthcare, Ontario, Canada. She had also worked in various Medical and Dental Universities across the globe in high academic positions and has earned laurel through her educational expertise.

Mental Health is a subject of deep interest for Prof. Usha. Healthy Living and Mental Health have direct relations with each other. As she explains- Life is full of experiences of happy and sad moments. Trauma, agonies, positivity, negativity, and pain are integral parts of life. At times, they confound our minds to the extent that minds get overwhelmed and baffled in dealing with them. This may culminate into different forms of psychological expression or mental illness, through diverse conditions like Anxiety disorder, Depression, PTSD, or panic attacks, at times, leading to destructive effects on our lives.

Prof. Usha states, 'Mental health is as much significant as the physical health of an individual. Our mental health directly determines the status of our overall health and wellbeing. Proper understanding and knowledge of Health and Wellness Continuum are vital issues in the modern life. Every one of us needs to understand and value the mental health.'

PRAISE FOR AUTHOR

I have had the pleasure of buying and enjoying the book, "The Deaths, lived all the way through".

Usha Dabas has gone where not a lot of authors, and for that matter, common folk, are scared to go- death. The ultimate reality that is death, is thoroughly explored in these 5 stories, with deep and emotional portrayal by the author. The stories struck a personal cord, especially "Rock Garden" paints a powerful portrayal of love- that knows no bounds, not even species.

I applaud Dabas for her excellent effort and sentimental delivery.

Congratulations on your latest literary venture.

5.0 out of 5 stars Great literary venture

- ADRIAN

BOOKS BY THIS AUTHOR

The Deaths, Lived All The Way Through: Based Upon True Incidents

The Deaths lived all the way through is a special memoir enlightening momentous aspect of life called "Death" as analyzed and experienced by a Medical Professional. Her medical practice provides her with impetus and opportunities to experience diverse colors of life and death through everyday encounter with diseases and demises. This book is a compilation of short stories based upon true events presenting heartfelt stories of untimely deaths due to breast cancer, meningitis and severe depression; pain of losing the beloved pet, and an emotive tale of the body donation.

The ultimate truth and absolute eventuality in Life is Death. Life and death are the two inseparable halves of our existences. Diversity in the outlook and the approaches of people around the world towards the phenomenon of death has been evaluated from time and time again. Philosophers are engaged with the knowledge exchange processes related to Death.
The proverbial 24 hours of each day provide every one with ample impetus and opportunities to experience the diverse colors of human life. How one grasps and feels each one essentially depicts individual sensitivity and emotional quotient. In life there are always undesirable things, so in order to feel better we just require to look at the life from another direction. However big the problem may have been, life is certainly bigger than the problem.